SPIRIT FORWARD

HOW I ENCOUNTERED THE SPIRIT OF JESUS

KEN SCHAAP

Spirit Forward: How I Encountered the Spirit of Jesus
© 2024 Ken Schaap

TABLE OF CONTENTS

SPIRIT FORWARD

HOW I ENCOUNTERED THE SPIRIT OF JESUS

AN UNEXPECTED ENCOUNTER

I was painting a bathroom when the Holy Spirit set me free. In April 2017, we worked on the latest home project, finishing our basement and installing a bathroom with a specialized bathtub to care for our son's special needs. I needed something to listen to as I worked my way around the small room with a roller and a brush. I had a habit back then of spending more time reading about prayer than time spent in actual prayer. The latest book I'd read had rocked me, though. It was *Surprised by the Power of the Holy Spirit,* by Dr. Jack Deere. Jack was a theologian, pastor, and professor in Biblical languages at Dallas Theological Seminary when a guest speaker visited his church, preached on the Kingdom of Heaven for three nights, and demonstrated the kingdom's power as if he were the Apostle Peter himself. Sick people were healed, actual words of knowledge were given, and the gift of prophecy was used to help dozens of people find freedom in Christ, all while Jack watched in disbelief.

So began his 10-year journey of discovering that there is more to be found in the Holy Spirit than the average Christian dares to imagine. Little did I know that by reading the book, my journey had just begun, too.

So there I was a couple of weeks after finishing the book, looking for something to listen to on YouTube while I painted. I found a video called "Casting Out Demons," by Jack Deere.[1] In it, Jack taught an informal lesson on the power of Jesus over the power of darkness, and then gave a simple invitation for people to come forward to receive prayer. There was nothing bombastic about his message. He told a few humorous stories, shared insight gained from dozens of deliverance sessions, and gave a simple, enjoyable message. Still, strangely, I found myself crying through it. I realized that I needed deliverance.

I was 32 years old, nearly three years into pastoring, a pastor's kid raised in church and made to sit through thousands of messages and lessons about the Bible. And yet I was discouraged, bound in lust, unable to break the final threads of a decades-long battle with pornography. I wallowed in shame, often seethed with anger, and was continually frustrated that I could not seem to break through in many areas of my life. Jack's simple lecture in that video turned a lightbulb on in my mind. I realized that through some of the painful experiences I had had in life, I had been wounded, and evil spirits had infected these wounds. In that realization, I felt no fear but rather love. I felt that Jesus was standing next to me, whispering in my ear truths about my heart and about the struggles I was enduring, tenderly making me aware that the battle was bigger than bad habits or besetting sin.

The video continued playing, and I continued my tearful painting. By this time, my wife, Candace, had joined me and was behind me painting another wall. Embarrassed by my tears, I said little to her and continued listening to the message. The prayer time at the end of Jack's message stretched on and didn't make for great listening. It was as if someone had left the mics on and left the audio booth. For about 15 minutes, there was a low sound of people receiving prayer; in some cases, crying could be heard.

---

1 Sometime in 2020 this video was taken down by the owner. I contacted him and asked for it, but he cannot find it.

I was deep in my own thoughts, not paying much attention anymore. Then I heard a tap on the mic and the gravelly voice of a different man. To this day, I'm not sure who it was. But I learned quickly that that man could pray! He prayed a prayer of declaration and power. He commanded evil spirits to flee and for chains to break. I could feel chains breaking off me and darkness departing from my soul. It was so tangible. My body began to tremble, and I began to weep. When I turned to face my wife, I was surprised to see that she, too, was weeping, overcome by the work of the Spirit in her own heart. We embraced. Still holding our paint rollers, we put our heads on each other's shoulders and let the pain and infection of perversion, betrayal, disappointment, and despair roll off of us, all while a 20-year-old video played the prayer of a man who we might never meet, but who clearly walked in the authority and power of King Jesus.

That day, I began life in the Spirit. The experiences of another man found in a book became my personal experience in the most unexpected of times and strangest of places. I encountered Jesus, and He changed me forever. [2]

This book is the story of how the Holy Spirit changed my life. He is the greatest gift that Abba Father ever gave me. The Holy Spirit introduced me to Jesus and drew me to salvation as a five-year-old boy. The Holy Spirit convicted me of sin thousands of times and drew me to the feet of a forgiving Father. The Holy Spirit touched my heart and called me into a life of prayer during a 40-day fast at age 21.

---

2 Incidentally, about three years later I was sitting down with Jerod Long, my lifelong friend and fellow elder at The Father's House. He was sharing with me the moment when God set him free from a lifelong struggle with lust and anger. "It was about three years ago," he said. "It was an old Jack Deere message about demons. The message was okay, but then a guy prayed at the end and I felt a burning in my stomach and felt spirits of perversion and lust leave me. Jesus set me free and cleansed my heart in that moment.
I was stunned. For all of the life experiences we've shared, we somehow never realized that we'd listened to the same message in the same month and had incredibly similar experiences. Craziness! That's how life in the Spirit goes, one incredible miracle after another.

But He was always in the background. His name was a name we used as a figure of speech to declare that things in the church were going well. "The Spirit is moving," we would say. Or, "The Holy Spirit sure took over that service." These phrases were typically used to describe a season in our church, a crowd's response to a powerful song, or a prayer time after a dynamic service. It wasn't until that basement bathroom experience with fresh paint on the walls that I realized I was completely ignorant of this Person from the Godhead that lived inside of me.

Nearly seven years later, my friend, the Holy Spirit of God, has compelled me to write this. My heart is full of a thousand stories of miracles, changed lives, victorious warfare, and answered prayers, all because He came in and touched my life. I hope in reading this book you'll open your heart to Him. It's likely that you already know Him, for He has been with you. (John 14:17) It's also likely that you've felt Him, for if you are born again, He is inside of you. (Ephesians 1:13) But perhaps, like me, you need His powerful presence to fall upon you. Perhaps a garment of heaviness weighs you down, robbing you of joy while trapping you in despair and cynicism. My prayer is that my stories and the prayers I've written in the following chapters will have the same effect on you as an old book and YouTube video had on me. I've added a prayer at the end of each chapter that I hope you'll pray out loud more than once, making it your own prayer from the heart. I know that some of the topics covered in these chapters may challenge your own traditions and beliefs. I only ask that you partner with the Holy Spirit and stick with it to the end of the book. I believe God has something very special in store for you.

May the eyes of your heart be enlightened, and may you know the love of Christ. May Jesus Himself walk into your heart and fill you with His mighty Spirit in ways you never imagined possible.

CHAPTER 1

POWER

> *John baptized with water but you will be baptized with the Holy Spirit.*
> Acts 1:5
>
> *And he said to them, "Did you receive the Holy Spirit when you believed? And they said, "No," we have not even heard that there is a Holy Spirit. And he said, "Into what then were you baptized?"*
> Acts 19:2-3

I come by this Holy Spirit obsession quite honestly. My grandfather, Jack Hyles, was an influential pastor who traveled throughout the United States preaching the Gospel of Jesus. He rubbed shoulders with Billy Graham, impacted Tommy Barnett,[3] and helped organize the fledgling Sunday school program of a young pastor named Jerry Falwell. In the 1970s, the First Baptist Church of Hammond, Indiana, was routinely recognized as

---

3 Tommy Barnett, long time pastor of the Dream Center in California, is an Assemblies of God pastor who was transformed at one of Hyles' Pastor's School conferences. Barnett eventually started his own "Pastors School" conferences, impacting hundreds of leaders worldwide. See Barnett, Tommy. *What If?* (p. 98). ARC Resources, Kindle Edition.

one of the largest churches in America. While he was known for many things, his emphasis on the Holy Spirit set him apart. Two of his most famous messages were entitled "Fresh Oil" and "This Kind." In them he shared personal testimonies that emphasized the miracle-working power of God. These stories formulated my faith as a young boy. Nearly every night of my childhood, I fell asleep listening to a cassette tape playing one of his sermons.

I heard incredible stories in those messages. He shared the story of praying for nearly two days on the fresh grave of his unsaved father, asking God for power so that no one who heard his preaching would ever leave without Christ. Thousands and thousands of people were saved under his preaching. It was not unusual for me to look down from my favorite balcony seat in that vast auditorium and see the entire front of the church packed with people who had come forward at the conclusion of a sermon to make a public confession of putting their faith in Christ.

There were miracle stories, too. A man who was completely blind for several years was healed in the middle of a Sunday morning service and walked onto the platform praising God. A woman diagnosed with a severe brain tumor had her surgery canceled after my grandfather anointed her with oil and prayed for healing.

My favorite miracle story, and one I vaguely remember as a six-year-old boy, was when, during one service, my grandfather stopped the typical service order because a family from our church had been in a terrible car wreck. One of the girls in the family had a broken neck, and her outlook was bleak. The church, filled with thousands of people, all bowed their heads while my grandfather prayed for her healing. New X-rays were taken an hour later. Her broken neck had been miraculously healed. That little girl was named Candace, and she's now my wife.

Based on the hundreds of sermons I heard as a child, there was little question in my mind that God's power still operated today. What wasn't as clear was who was allowed to operate in this power. The first and most obvious one was the man behind the pulpit. My Grandpa Hyles was "the man of God." His life story was gripping, and he told portions of it nearly every week.[4] He was raised in poverty in a single-parent home in east Texas, abandoned by an alcoholic father, and drafted into the army at the end of World War II, where he was trained as a paratrooper. His mother was portrayed as a tirelessly working heroic prayer warrior.

To hear him tell it, her prayers kept him from alcohol, her prayers kept him from seeing action as the war wound down, and her prayers opened his heart to the call of full-time ministry. He started in the pastorate as a 20-year-old man taking a church with 19 members. Three churches later, he was leading the fastest-growing church in America in Garland, Texas. Then God moved him. A church in Indiana with 700 members called him, and he labored over the decision. His stories about the move made it clear to me that God spoke to him. He saw signs that confirmed the move and had conversations in prayer with God where he argued about making the move. Upon making the move and taking the pastorate, the church exploded in growth. The attendance grew from 700 in 1960 to 12,000 by 1975. The church started a college to be a ministry training center. Multiple private schools were started. He was a man filled with charisma and passion for God. I did not doubt that God could do mighty things through him.

But what about me? How exactly did God's power work? Was it just for the pastor or an exceptional man of God?

For all of my Grandpa's stories, there wasn't very much systematized teaching on the doctrine of God's power. The church was encouraged to pray for it, but I still wasn't sure if there was anything else I should be doing. The gifts of the Spirit were rarely mentioned, and instructions on operating in partnership with the Holy Spirit were no longer taught.

---

4 Most of these stories are captured in his biography, written by my Mom, Cindy Hyles Collins. *The Fundamental Man*. 1998, Hyles Publications, Hammond, Indiana.

By the time I moved my family to Ohio and started a church, my grandfather had been dead for over 12 years. In that time, I'd learned the other side. His successor had inherited a church after his death, facing over 30 lawsuits. Scandals that had been mostly covered up started coming out through social media. The perversion, the broken people, and the cover-ups I learned about left me reeling. It seemed that the first half of his ministry seemed marked with Holy Spirit power and explosive growth, and the second half with scandals and survival. The church went on after his death, but more scandals and accusations surfaced until a new scandal threatened its very survival. The successor to my grandfather had initially helped the church rebound to new growth, but an economic downturn deeply impacted the finances, and layoffs began. Shortly after, it was discovered that the pastor had been engaged in an affair with a teenager in the church. It was not only a grievous sin but a federal crime. The community went into an uproar, and the media went into a frenzy.

To make matters worse, this successor guilty of this crime was someone I admired even more than my grandfather. He was my spiritual hero. He was my Dad.[5]

Sixteen years after my Grandfather's passing and five years after my father's imprisonment, I held my wife, weeping the tears of a man set free. God was doing something new in my life. I was hungry for His power again. The Holy Spirit had touched me. I'd had an experience, the first of many. But what exactly had happened, and was there Scripture to support it?

THE PRESENCE AND POWER OF THE HOLY SPIRIT ON JESUS

The Holy Spirit is all over the Gospel of Luke.

- John the Baptist, the Forerunner for Jesus, is filled with the Holy Spirit from his mother, Elizabeth's womb. (Luke 1:15)

---

5 More on that in Chapter 8 (Forgiveness).

- Elizabeth herself, a woman past childbearing years, conceives a child with her husband and is also filled with the Holy Spirit. (Luke 1:14)

- Zechariah, Elizabeth's husband, is filled with the Spirit. and prophesies at the birth of John. (Luke 1:67)

- Mary, the Mother of Jesus, is overshadowed by the Holy Spirit in her virginity, conceiving and then carrying our Lord. (Luke 1:35) While pregnant, her prayer is definitive evidence of ongoing Spirit fullness. (Luke1:46-55)

- If John the Baptist is Spirit-filled before birth, it's safe to say that Jesus was also.

- Old Man Simeon was filled with the Spirit as He waited for the arrival of the Messiah. (Luke 2:25-26)

- John the Baptist declares the coming Messiah will baptize His followers in the Holy Spirit. (Luke 3:16)

- The Spirit descends in the bodily form of a dove upon Jesus at His baptism. (Luke 3:22)

- Jesus is filled with the Spirit and led by the Spirit into the wilderness for The Temptation. (Luke 4:1)

- For the first time, we see the Power of the Spirit as Jesus returns from the temptation. (Luke 4:14)

- Jesus declares that He is the fulfillment of Isaiah 61's powerful declaration, "The Spirit of the Lord is upon me." (Luke 4:18-21)

From there, the authority and power of Jesus are on full display.

- He teaches with unprecedented authority. (Luke 4:32)
- He heals multitudes and casts out demons. (Luke 4:36-41)
- He calls the disciples in prophetic power and authority. (Luke 5:1-11)

- He heals lepers and paralytics and forgives sins! (Luke 5:12-26)

In summary, after being conceived of the Holy Spirit, Jesus is filled with the Spirit from birth, baptized in the Spirit, and led of the Spirit into a wilderness temptation from which He returns in the power (and authority) of the Spirit.

THE BAPTISM OF THE SPIRIT FOR JESUS AND FOR BELIEVERS

I believe this is clearly the template for our relationship and interactions with the Holy Spirit:

> We are born again as a work of the Holy Spirit (John 3:5-6) and filled with the Holy Spirit from that new birth. (Ephesians 1:13) We are then able to go to Jesus, drawn by His Spirit, to be baptized by the Spirit.

After this baptism, we are able to resist temptation like never before and to walk in greater power and authority than ever before.

Go back and read the previous sentence one more time. Now, read it again. Okay, I'll write it out again for you here: "After this baptism, we are able to resist temptation like never before and to walk in greater power and authority than ever before."

Is it any wonder that "the baptism of the Spirit is a theological controversy?" According to the pattern set by Jesus, it is evident that without the baptism of the Spirit, we are not fully ready to endure the Tempter. The process of Christ's progression in the Spirit is not a coincidence. Jesus is…

…Conceived by the Spirit…Filled from birth with the Spirit… Baptized in the Spirit…Untainted by Satan in the Temptation…Moving in the power and authority of the Spirit.

Many in the church ignore the clear pattern set by our Lord's example. They assume the baptism comes simultaneously with the New Birth.

No wonder we have so many Christians in the Body who are filled with perversion. They are in the wilderness, vulnerable and defenseless because they have not experienced the baptism!

I certainly believe that the New Birth and the Baptism of the Spirit can be the same event, but the Scriptures plainly show that they can also happen at distinctly *separate* times. The main reason for this is because of ignorance. In Acts 2:38, Peter preaches the Gospel of repentance while explaining the promise of the Holy Spirit. Those who believe immediately receive the Spirit. However, the Samaritans (Acts 8), Apollos (Acts 18), and the Ephesians (Acts 19:1-6) are all examples of believers who were born again but still in need of the baptism of the Spirit.

I, too, am a witness of this. I was in a church that loved Jesus and had many Spirit-filled believers, so the Holy Spirit was *with* me. I was born again at age five, and from then on, the Holy Spirit was *in* me. However, it was not until I was 31 that I was baptized in the Spirit, at which point He was *on* me. I pray that you will continue with me in this book and see the evidence of the Holy Spirit's work in my life.

> *Why is it that some Christians are uneasy at the thought that there may be more for them after their conversion? Is it something they don't want to think about? Is it something that would challenge their theology? Or pride? Does the idea of a baptism, or sealing, of the Spirit beyond conversion suggest they would have to move out of their comfort zones? Or is it not a thrilling possibility— that of experiencing the power, the peace, and joy from the immediate witness of the Holy Spirit?*[6] – R.T. Kendall

---

6 Kendall, R.T. *Holy Fire: A Balanced, Biblical Look at the Holy Spirit's Work in Our Lives* (p. 199). Charisma House, Kindle Edition.

TRYING TO FIGURE OUT WHAT HAPPENED TO ME?

The challenge for me was that I wasn't totally sure of what had happened to me. I had no older mentors in my life that I could call. Even if I did, I'm unsure what I would have said. *"I was painting a bathroom, an old man prayed on YouTube, I sobbed like a baby, and now I don't struggle with discouragement or lust anymore."*

One issue was I'd been keeping my struggles mostly secret. I'd fought with lust and the pornography that fed it for twenty years. There were lengthy seasons where I'd be victorious, but there seemed to be these internal triggers in me that the enemy knew how to get to and flip eventually. With unresolved lust comes anger. I had a primarily internal rage that kept me in seasons of brooding darkness with occasional fiery outbursts or controlling actions of manipulation.

On top of that was a deep discouragement and, if I'm being honest, depression that sat on me like a heavy darkness. Anxiety kept me awake in the night and exhausted during the day. The wounds of disappointment over my father and my own obvious inadequacies as a husband and pastor had been bringing me down. But my one virtue was I kept moving forward. Painfully slow, one step after another, I pushed ahead through financial struggles, severe criticism, and false accusations while crying out to God. Jesus is faithful. He knew what I needed. I needed the Holy Spirit to come upon me and all the fruit and gifts that life with Him reveals.

In the days after that encounter, I felt a peace I'd never realized was possible. I had drunk something that actually satisfied me. I'd found the buried treasure, the pearl of great price, the lost coin I'd been searching for. I was in awe. My wife noticed a difference in me, and I in her. Our home was different. My usually dull prayer time was suddenly vibrant. What had happened, and how could I keep it? It was a gift. How could I steward it?

(A prayer for anyone who hungers for a fresh touch from God.)

Father,

I pray in the mighty name of Jesus that you would pour your Holy Spirit on me in a fresh and tangible way. I pray that I would have a fresh experience of your infinite love, a transformative glimpse of your indescribable Glory, and an undeniable encounter with your beautiful presence. Baptize me with your Spirit and with your Holy Fire.

Holy Spirit, I receive you now. Come, rest upon me like a dove. Whisper to me in my inner man. Open the eyes of my heart to the beauty of Jesus and the Glory of the Father.

Amen

CHAPTER 2

HOLY GHOST HIGH

> *"And suddenly there came from heaven a sound like a mighty*
> *rushing wind, and it filled the entire house where they were sitting.*
> *And divided tongues as of fire appeared to them and rested on each*
> *one of them. And they were all filled with the Holy Spirit and began*
> *to speak in other tongues as the Spirit gave them utterance."*
> (Acts 2:2–4, ESV)

Soon after my encounter with the Spirit, I was working in the yard at the church where I pastor, assembling a play set for our children's ministry. As I worked, a car came recklessly speeding through the parking lot, screeching to a halt on the other side of the building. As I took a moment to think about what I should do, I heard sirens and saw three police cars quickly coming down the street, heading toward our little neighborhood church. I sprinted over to where all the action was. I arrived in time to see an officer pull a man from the back seat of the first car that I had seen. The man was completely naked with a needle stuck in his right thigh. He appeared to be dead, and his body was now lying on the pavement of my church parking lot while two officers crouched over him, attempting to revive him.

Needless to say, I was stunned. At the time, I was a pastor in West Chester, a proud suburb north of Cincinnati, Ohio. It's a relatively affluent area, and there isn't much violent crime. What I was seeing was not a common occurrence in our community. Though I'd done many years of inner city work in Chicago and seen violence and drug abuse up close and personal, this scene before me was still a first.

Soon, an ambulance arrived and took the man away, who thankfully survived. As I stood there speaking with the officers, I was struck by the thought, "Our community doesn't have any answers for this. I'm not sure I have any answers for this. Holy Spirit, how would you fix this?"

Illicit drugs like heroin have ravaged our State and much of America from coast to coast and throughout the Midwest. Despite the thousands of rehabilitation organizations and religious ministries dedicated to recovery and freedom, cases of addiction and the accompanying terrible consequences continue to rise. My brother-in-law, Matt, is one of the "lucky ones." After spiraling deeply into a life of addiction in his 20s, God used the recovery ministry of my home church to help him find freedom. Within a few years, Matt took over the program as director. We talked regularly about the frustration that came with it. The success rate for long-term recovery was below 10 percent. As I pondered the craziness of the scene I had just witnessed, I heard or, rather felt, a voice inside of me say, "I showed you this for a reason. Finish Jackie's book."

Upon completing Jack Deere's "Surprised by the Power" book, the next one on my list was a missionary story, "Chasing the Dragon" by Jackie Pullinger. After the "Surprised" book, I didn't think anything else could rock me. I was wrong. I've read thousands of books in my life. Most of them had little effect. But in this season, it was as if the Holy Spirit was choosing my books for me and using one at a time to break open my heart and make room for Him.

CHASING THE DRAGON

Jackie Pullinger was a single woman who, upon graduating from school, began to hear a recurring word from the Lord that simply was, "Go." Each time she heard it, she responded that she would go wherever if only He would show her. After several weeks, she met with her pastor, who reminded her of the Lord's word to Abraham: "Go to a land which I will show thee."

So Jackie booked passage on a freighter with over a dozen different ports on its route worldwide. At each stop, she asked the Lord, "Is this it? Is this where you want me to be?" Finally, as they arrived in port in Hong Kong, He responded to her prayer that she had arrived at her new home.

She stepped off the boat as a missionary. She had no husband, financial support, backing of any church or denomination, and very little training. She knew little about China and was utterly ignorant about Kowloon's Walled City. At that time, the Walled City was a lawless, ungoverned, seven-acre tenement of hastily built buildings filled with 50,000 residents, with no electricity, no running water (until later), and only one toilet. Chinese gangs called Triads oversaw the entire area and peddled opioids and pimped prostitutes of any age.

Jackie says she felt incredible joy as she stepped into the darkness of the city. A supernatural energy from the Lord assured her she was in the right place. She would need it. For months, her evangelization attempts fell on deaf ears or were met with mockery and skepticism. This place of no police, no order, and no rules seemed like a place that even Jesus wouldn't visit. But she persisted. A Christian school just outside the city kicked out a 14-year-old boy because he was too old and they were out of room, so to survive, he moved into an opium den, where he peddled drugs and cared for the young slave girls each morning after their latest customer had abused them. Broken-hearted by the realization that there was no future for these teenagers, Jackie started a youth club in a little room in the city. Outside the club was an open sewer running down the street, with addicts scouring through it in hopes of finding some lost coin to help them purchase their next fix. Her club was also a neighbor to 40 opium and heroin dens and a dozen brothels. Yet, in her little room, the youth found a little haven from it all. They played ping-pong, threw darts, ate candy, and barely tolerated Jackie's Bible lessons. This was not enough for Jackie. These teens were not encountering Jesus, and it ate at her. She described herself in that season as being patiently impatient. She could be patient for God to use her, but she was impatient as she watched young men and women's lives spiral toward complete destruction.

An elderly Chinese couple found her one day and invited her to dinner to pray and receive the Holy Spirit. Jackie was offended. Her conversion experience years before had marked her. It had been a powerful encounter with the Lord, and within days, she had shared the Gospel with a friend and become a passionate evangelist. She had the Holy Spirit, and any suggestion otherwise in her mind was ignorant at best and heretical at worst. But to avoid being rude, she had dinner with this couple. After dinner, they lit some candles, sang a song, smeared some oil on Jackie's forehead, and began to pray that she would receive the Spirit. Jackie had heard enough and was ready to leave, but when she opened her mouth, a language came out that was both beautiful and mysterious. She had read 1 Corinthians 12-14 and knew of the gift of tongues, but had never desired it or found any value in it. Now she had it. Embarrassed, she quickly left the couple's home, planning to never speak to them again. Dutifully, she thanked the Lord in private devotions for giving her a gift, but she did nothing with it. It was so embarrassing, even in private. It made her feel foolish and did nothing for her emotionally. Yet, the Lord would not let it go. Months later, an American missionary visited and pulled Jackie aside, asking her if she prayed in tongues. She admitted that it felt useless and weird. The American urged her to persist and dedicate 30 minutes of daily praying in this unknown language. Feeling as though this was from the Lord, Jackie complied. Day after day, she felt little change, but continued exercising this gift. But, as gradually as a season changes, like Spring to Summer, Jackie's ministry shifted. She found herself on a bench just outside the city with a boy named Christopher from her youth club. He was in despair over the pointlessness of life. Once again, Jackie began to share a Gospel plan that had had no effect over the last two years. Christopher encountered Jesus dramatically and, within a few days, would bring several other boys to the Youth Club to hear about Jesus from Jackie. Strangely, though Jackie did not teach or speak openly about tongues, the boys broke out in tongues, many of them immediately after being saved. These were boys who lived as orphans sleeping in the opium dens and on the streets, most already addicted to a narcotic of some sort. As she ministered to them, Jackie was stunned to see several *immediately* detox from the drugs while praying in tongues.

One night, a brand new follower of Christ freshly delivered from heroin felt an impression from the Spirit and began to give the word from the Lord in tongues. As he finished, Christopher began to sing the interpretation. This is what he sang:

Oh God, who saves me in the darkness,

Give me strength and the power

So I can walk in the Holy Spirit

Fight against the devil with the Bible

Talk to the sinners in the world

Make them belong to Christ.

Another boy, Bobby, had the same interpretation but in Chinese. He did not understand Christopher's English song, so he did not know that what he spoke was a confirmation of God's message. The Spirit was moving mightily, and this little fortress of darkness would never be the same.

Now, over 50 years later, Jackie can point to tens of thousands of addicts who have been set free by Jesus, saved, and filled with the Holy Spirit through her ministry. China eventually tore down the Walled City and gave Jackie some land to continue her work, recognizing her as having an 85% success rate with the addicted. Privately, Jackie disagrees. It's more like 100%. Jesus never loses anyone who receives Him.

HOW DO I KEEP IT?

I read the book in one evening, the graphic image of the overdosed dying man lying on my church pavement resting in the back of my mind. Jackie's stories had their own wild imagery—a single white British lady in one of the darkest places on earth helping the poor and the addicted find freedom through the Gospel and the Holy Spirit.

But what about this issue of tongues?

Ever since my encounter, I'd been asking the Lord how to keep and steward this new joy. You see, I'd experienced something like this before as a much younger man and then lost it. At 21 years of age, after reading a book entitled "Deeper Experiences of Famous Christians," I began a 40-day fast from solid food. I was a preacher without power, a husband without a clue, and a man without understanding. I was so disappointed in whom I was, and I was desperate for God. I lost nearly 50 pounds and most of my hair, but I found the Lord for myself. After finishing the fast, the Bible and prayer became my passion, and I felt a profound sense of joy and confidence in the Lord. But it went away. The old struggles of the flesh flared back up, and I fell into mediocrity. I was a lukewarm Christian again.

As a 33-year-old man, I found myself again filled with God-given joy and peace. "Holy Spirit, how can I keep it this time?"

"You're going to need tongues," He said.

"I THOUGHT TONGUES STOPPED A LONG TIME AGO"

Again, with my church experience being only Baptist, I had little understanding and no experience with the Gift of Tongues. Everything I had heard about it was terrible. There'd been some video clips of televangelists spewing gibberish with eyes tightly closed and fists raised. It had weirded me out. My teachers in Bible college said nothing much about it other than what it was has passed, and what people say it is now isn't what it was. The company line went something like this: "Tongues will cease." They quoted from Scripture before going on. "The Bible says that when "the perfect has come," there won't be any more need for tongues. We have God's perfect Word. We don't need tongues, and people who use tongues today are deceived."

After reading Jackie's book, I mulled over the standard objections against tongues I'd been taught. "The Bible says that when we get the Bible, we won't need tongues." It seemed like a contradictory argument. However, I knew that the enemy is a masterful deceiver. I knew the encounters I'd had could possibly be from the enemy. I still had quite a bit of religious fear in me. So I turned to the Bible, the Book that has so often saved me from myself along with the troubles of this world.

In my childhood home, I had the only bedroom upstairs. Nearly every morning of my life, I would wake up and descend the stairs to the same picture. My mom would be sitting on a recliner in the living room, reading her Bible while holding a coffee mug. My dad would be sitting at the head of the kitchen table, Bible opened before him and a mug of coffee nearby. Years later, my mornings always start in a similar way, a Yeti mug filled with coffee, and a continuation of my journey for the umpteenth time through the Scriptures.

The Bible is such a precious gift from the Lord. It's His revelation to us and, I've discovered, His validation or rejection of any other revelation we might receive. The Bible promises us that God still speaks, and it then serves as a standard to help us know whether what we are hearing is from God or not.

I felt called by the Lord to ask for the gift of tongues, which was a severe challenge to all that I'd learned in my upbringing. But I realized I'd never studied it out for myself. I'd never actually considered what the Bible said about this topic. What I discovered was surprising.

THE GIFT OF TONGUES AND THE DISCIPLINE OF PRAYING IN THE SPIRIT

I felt like I had dozens of questions bouncing through my head during that season, but four that the Scriptures answered very clearly moved me ahead in my journey with the Spirit.

- What is the Gift of Tongues?
- What's the point of it? Or, What purpose did it serve those who used it?
- When does it stop?
- If it hasn't stopped, how do I get it?

WHAT IS THE GIFT OF TONGUES?

The Gift of Tongues is one of the nine spiritual gifts mentioned by the Apostle Paul in I Corinthians 12. When the Holy Spirit was poured out on the Church at Pentecost (Acts 2), the 120 believers began to speak in "other tongues." Individuals from 15 different cultures are mentioned in Acts 2:7-11 as being able to hear the native language of home being spoken by these newly Spirit-filled believers. The believers were "given utterance" by the Spirit to declare "the mighty works of God" in languages that they had never learned.

If Acts 2 were the only text we had on the topic of tongues, we wouldn't have much to go on. Are they praying here? (Pentecostals would say yes.)

Are they preaching? (Baptists would prefer this answer.) Whatever they're doing here, this "sign" of tongues continues to appear in the Book of Acts.

In Acts 8, the apostles led by Peter lay hands on a group of new believers and "they received the Holy Spirit."[7] The chapter continues by indicating that people could see that the Holy Spirit had been received. What visual indication was there? The chapter doesn't say, but other stories in Acts give us additional insight.

In Acts 10, Peter along with three friends, is called to a Roman soldier's home where he preaches the Gospel to the entire household. The Bible says they were amazed because they could see that the Holy Spirit had fallen on the household, "For they were hearing them speaking in tongues and extolling God." [8]

In Acts 19, Paul lays his hands on some new believers at Ephesus and "the Holy Spirit came on them, and they began speaking in tongues."[9]

As I finished my study of tongues in the Book of Acts, one issue I had was that tongues was always mentioned as a sign for new believers who were receiving the Spirit. Once you were no longer a "new" believer, was tongues still a gift that you were to use? It seemed that everyone who received the gift either prayed or at least declared praise to God or appreciation for some great work He had done. "Did they know what they were saying?" I wondered.

Having some basic understanding of the principles of Bible interpretation, I know the Book of Acts is a historical book, and because history is often subject to interpretation, thereby causing disagreement, additional resources were needed. My study continued in I Corinthians 12 and 14.

In I Corinthians 12, the Apostle Paul gives a list of special gifts or abilities that come as a result of the Ministry of the Holy Spirit in the life

---

7 Acts 8:17.
8 Acts 10:45.
9 Acts 19:6.

of a believer. One of his points in writing it is to show the diversity of the Body of Christ. Everyone has different gifts, and each gift is needed. As I read it with fresh eyes, I was struck by how the attitude of many churches was contrary to this. Their stance seemed to be that not every gift was needed or at least wanted. "Keep tongues out of this church" seemed to be a prevalent attitude in church circles in which I'd been raised.

I Corinthians 14 is the most detailed explanation of tongues found in Scripture. The Church at Corinth was abusing the gifts by drawing attention to themselves rather than bringing glory to God, and in doing so was creating quite a bit of confusion. Pride seemed to be their motivation, rather than love. These special and sacred spiritual gifts that the church had received were being turned into points of boasting. The church had a dark underbelly, too. There was in-fighting as well as grievous sexual immorality present in the congregation.

It's in this context that Paul writes his letter. In chapter 14, Paul takes two spiritual gifts and contrasts them to show how care and service for the church should be prioritized above self-care regardless of how spiritual it sounds or looks. In the times past when I had read this chapter with a built-in bias against tongues, it had been easy for me to see Paul speaking negatively about this gift.

"One who speaks in a tongue builds up himself…"

"If you utter unintelligible speech how will anyone know what is said? You will be speaking into the air?"

"I would rather speak five words with my mind to instruct others, than ten thousand words in a tongue."

It sure seemed to me from verses like these that tongues were a "no-go" anymore for today's Christian. They seemed to be evidences of pride, sources of confusion, and vain repetitions. But I still had to do something about the very strong voice in my spirit that was telling me to *pursue* this gift. Though I felt uncertain, I did have the clear word of admonition from Paul to "earnestly desire spiritual gifts" and despite all the negative I was seeing, the Gift of Tongues was still in the list of gifts. So I took another look at chapter 14, and this time it was like I only saw the good.[10]

"One who speaks in a tongue speaks unto God and utters mysteries in the Spirit." (14:2)

"The one who speaks in a tongue builds himself up...Now I want you all to speak in tongues." (14:4-5)

"If I pray in a tongue, my spirit prays but my mind is unfruitful...I will pray with my spirit, but I will pray with my mind, also; I will sing praise with my spirit, but I will sing with my mind also." (14:14-15)

"I thank God that I speak in tongues more than all of you." (14:18)

"If there is no one (at church) to interpret, speak (tongues) to (yourself) and to God." (14:28)

"Do not forbid speaking in tongues." (14:39)

What is the gift of tongues? Also referred to as "praying in the Spirit,"[11] this gift is the act of speaking words from the spirit that your mind does not understand. These words in other languages declare praises, prayers, and even mysteries to God. I finally had my answer to my first question.

WHAT'S THE POINT OF IT? OR, WHAT PURPOSE DID IT SERVE THOSE WHO USED IT?

I Corinthians had definitely addressed any questions that had come from the Book of Acts. This gift was not just a *sign*. It was a resource for strength and revelation. Praying in the Spirit makes you stronger. Paul said it builds you up and Jude said that it builds up your faith. I firmly believe that one reason we "lose" the fire of spiritual experiences is because our faith grows weak due to a lack of prayer, specifically a lack of praying in tongues. God

---

10 To be clear, this study took place over several weeks along with several conversations with my friend and fellow elder, Jerod Long.

11 I Corinthians 14:14-15, Ephesians 6:18, Jude 20.

answers prayer, but sometimes we don't know what to pray for. It's in these moments (which are many more than we realize) that we need this gift.

Praying in the Spirit reveals truths from God's heart. Paul made known more mysteries of God's heart than any other person aside from Jesus.[12] One reason for this is because he prayed in tongues more than anyone else.

I don't know about you, but I could certainly use stronger faith, and more insight into the mind and heart of God.

WHEN DOES IT STOP?

At this point in my study, I was pretty excited. There was much more to this gift than I'd ever realized, but I still had one major obstacle. Doesn't the Bible say this gift stopped? I found it in I Corinthians 13:8,10 "…As for tongues, they will cease…When the perfect comes…"

What's the perfect? When is it coming, or has it already come? I knew enough about the topic to know there were two main opinions about this. The opinion I was taught in my training was that the perfect was the Bible, and with the completion of the New Testament and not coincidentally the passing of the 12 apostles, the miraculous spiritual gifts like healing, prophecy, words of knowledge, and, yes, tongues (along with interpretation of tongues) had gone away.

The other opinion that I saw in different resources I read was that the perfect was referring to the consummation of the Kingdom of God. When at His return, Jesus sits on a throne on Mount Zion as King of Kings over all the Earth, the age we are now living in will be complete. As I studied further, I realized the Bible has a lot to say about the return of Christ. I mean hundreds of verses. Conversely, the Bible has nothing to say about the completion of the Bible or the significance of the passing of the apostles.

---

12 See I Corinthians 2:6,12,13.

One rule of interpreting Scripture is to always keep context in mind as you study. One rule of context is to consider what the author has to say about his own writing. If I have a question about what Paul wrote, the best place to look is to the rest of Paul's writing to see if he answers the question in any other of his writings. The question, then, was did Paul write anything else that answered what "the perfect" was. I found it in I Corinthians 1:7. Paul thanked God that He would enrich the church at Corinth so that they would not be "lacking in any gift, as they wait for the revealing of our Lord Jesus Christ." The King James Version translates it as "the coming of our Lord Jesus Christ."

Here it was. Paul gave an *"until."* The next event that the Corinthian church was waiting for was the revealing of Jesus at His return. We are living in the "partial" while waiting on the "perfect." The "partial" that we live in now is a portion of the Kingdom that began breaking into this world at the Resurrection of Jesus and outpouring of the Spirit at Pentecost.

When will the Gift of Tongues pass away? When Jesus returns to this earth as King. At this point, He will reveal the mysteries of the Father "face to face."

IF IT HASN'T STOPPED, HOW DO I GET IT?

The Holy Spirit had convinced me. This gift was still happening today. Jackie Pullinger's stories were very likely true. People were being instantly delivered from drug addiction, being saved, and breaking out unprompted in this incredible gift. So, how do I get this gift?

Thankfully the answer to this one wasn't too difficult. Ask for it.

Luke 7:11 *If you then, who are evil, know how to give good gifts to your children, how much more will your Father who is in Heaven give good things to those who ask Him!*

It couldn't be this simple. Just ask? I'll never forget the day I went into the spare bedroom of our home and laid face-down on my sheepskin prayer rug, opened my Bible to this passage and, after reading it out loud, began to pray.

"Father, I want the gift of tongues. Even after everything I've read, I still have a fear of inviting something demonic. But I know from experience and from your Word that I can trust you. If I ask you for a fish, you won't give me a snake. If I ask you for bread, you won't give me a stone. If I ask you for tongues you won't give me a demon. You've already given me so much through the Holy Spirit. According to your Word, I repent of the disrespectful and grievous things that I have said about this gift and I ask you to bless me with it."

I opened my mouth. Listened for an inner voice. Breathed out a sigh of submission and began to search for whatever the spirit had for me. *"….mmm….ahhhh….agabathe."* From there, a string of syllables came forth and I wept as these syllables poured out. I had no idea what they meant, but I felt the peace of God wash over me in fresh ways as I prayed in the Spirit.

SEEING THE FRUIT OF THIS GIFT

Even after the powerful experience I had in my prayer closet, I still wasn't sure what exactly to do with this gift. How often should I use it? Should I tell anyone? Candace had been with me on most of this journey, but she hadn't exactly read everything I'd read, and when I mentioned tongues, she didn't seem too thrilled about it. We were not ignorant of the fact that this gift was divisive and incredibly controversial. We were already experiencing some strange things. We certainly didn't need to upset our church and mention this gift.

I asked the Holy Spirit for help. What did the activation of this gift in my life mean? Would it be something that I just kept to myself? Ultimately, I told Candace about it and she smiled and basically said, "That's great… for you." I got the impression she wasn't interested.

I continued to ask the Lord for other confirmations. Part of Jackie Pullinger's testimony was that the Gospel had not borne much fruit for her until she had begun to pray in tongues. I brought it up to the Lord. The church where I pastor is small. Getting unsaved people to visit has always been a struggle. We saw people saved occasionally out on visitation, but five months into 2017, we'd seen fewer than three people saved all year. The week after I first began praying in tongues, I received a call. A man named Ryan needed help. His marriage was on the rocks and he had attempted suicide three different times, only for the Lord to stop it each time. Chains for hanging himself had strangely snapped under the weight of his body. A gun had refused to fire, twice, while pointed at his head. When aimed at the wall, it fired just fine.

I asked Ryan if he was saved. He insisted that he was, but shortly thereafter, he bowed his head and trusted Christ. Seeing a difference in her husband, Ryan's wife, Kelley, came to church the next week. At the end of the service, I led her to the Lord and she was born again. Soon their two children would be saved as well. Over the next eight weeks, with no visitation happening or pushes for guests in a church averaging 40 in attendance, 44 people were saved in our services. Each one was personally led to the Lord by me. I'm an intercessor, a preacher, somewhat prophetic, but I'm not a great evangelist. This gift of tongues seemed to work! What next, Lord?

> *The gospel must be preached with the involvement of the Holy Spirit sent down from heaven.*[13]
>
> – Jim Cymbala

---

13 Cymbala, Jim. *Fresh Wind, Fresh Fire: What Happens When God's Spirit Invades the Heart of His People* (p. 138). Zondervan,, Kindle Edition.

That same month, a lady from my home church drove down with the strangest of requests. Her older sister had died from an aneurysm in her brain, and it left her crippled with fear. In addition, recent scans of her own brain showed some disturbing spots. Though she attended a great church, the Lord prompted her to drive four hours for the elders of my church to pray for her. After a Sunday service on Memorial Day weekend, we gathered in my office, anointed her with oil, and began to pray. My friend and fellow elder, Jerod, prayed first out loud while I prayed silently. Then it was my turn. I prayed for her out loud while Jerod prayed silently.

The lady for whom we prayed is alive and healthy today. Free from any anxiety or spots on the brain. Hallelujah!

A few days later, Jerod called me. "Something happened while you were praying out loud in the office last Sunday," he said. "I went to pray under my breath while you were praying out loud, but English didn't come out. God gave me the gift of tongues!"

We rejoiced together. God was up to something special! What would He do next?

> *No ordinary human vocabulary can find the terminology to articulate my joy and the gratitude I feel for all God is for me in Jesus. My prayer language provides me with a means of giving heartfelt expression to these deeply personal and intimate affections for my Savior.*[14]
>
> – Dr. Sam Storms

---

14 Storms, Sam. *The Language of Heaven: Crucial Questions About Speaking in Tongues* (p. 80). Charisma House, Kindle Edition.

HOW TO LOSE FRIENDS IF YOU'RE A BAPTIST

A friend who pastored out East called. He was depressed. Years of leading a church that didn't want to follow him had worn him down. His therapist called him a severe case. His doctor had him on five prescriptions. His wife was very sick. His children were disillusioned with the faith. My friend was ready to quit. "You don't have the Holy Spirit," I told him.[15]

I knew he was a conservative Baptist and that what I was about to tell him would contradict much of what he believed about the Holy Spirit, but I plowed on ahead, feeling a surge from the Holy Spirit inside of me. I testified, told him about Jack Deere and Jackie Pullinger, and then prayed for him over the phone, ending the prayer with several phrases of praying in the Spirit. I'd never let another person hear me pray in tongues. I felt extremely embarrassed and quickly finished the call. Four hours later, he called me back. "What the heck did you do to me?" he asked. "I've been praying in Chinese ever since you hung up!"

Within a few months and with his doctor's approval, five years of taking five different medicines for his mental health stopped. He went down to one medication, and then eventually to none. God healed his mental illness through praying in tongues. I was elated, overwhelmed, and amazed by God all simultaneously.

Something my friend mentioned during our conversation stuck with me and bothered me. While struggling with his mental illness, he had called the most prominent leader in the Baptist movement, of which my home church was a part. That leader had told him that hundreds of pastors he worked with were also struggling with mental illness and were taking medication for it, including himself. There was no spiritual option given and no mention of the Holy Spirit. Instead, he gave him a referral to a psychiatrist.

---

15 I've learned to say this in a more theologically accurate way, but in this season, I said it this way a lot and the Lord blessed it despite the abrasiveness of it.

The Holy Spirit broke my heart that night. There are hundreds of pastors who deny the Baptism of the Spirit while mocking the gift of tongues and forbidding any practice of it. Yet they are struggling with severe mental illness to the point of needing medication while keeping it hidden from their congregations. Being on medication for mental illness is not shameful or a sin. I was indeed headed that way with the despair I felt. Then, the Holy Spirit interrupted a painting session and set me free. Since then, I've seen dozens of people receive prayer and, after consulting with their doctors, stop taking their medications, their minds at peace thanks to the power of the Holy Spirit.[16]

> *We're living as starving beggars, and we don't even know it. We spend millions of dollars on counseling and self-help, yet we see so little fruit in our lives. We wear ourselves out with religious activity, and still we find ourselves trapped in cycles of fear, depression, rejection, and self-hatred. As a result, we turn to comfort zones of overindulgence found in alcohol, entertainment, food, ungodly relationships—all of this to run from the poverty of our souls. At some point, each of us has to take an honest look at our lives and ask: Where is the breakdown? If I have been given the fullness of the life of God, why don't I experience it?*[17]
>
> – Evangelist Corey Russell

---

16 Some mental illness is indeed an illness and only medical care can help. In other cases, the illness is demonic, and deliverance brings freedom. Still other cases are related to a wounded and burnt-out heart. The fruit of the Spirit that comes in an encounter is often all that's needed, as was the case for my friend. Doctors and medicine are a tremendous grace in our culture, and I'm thankful for those who follow Jesus and help their patients not become solely dependent on medication.

17 Russell, Corey. *The Glory Within: The Interior Life and the Power of Speaking in Tongues* (p. 40). Destiny Image, Kindle Edition.

A PRAYER FOR HOLY GHOST POWER AND SPIRITUAL GIFTS

Father, in the name of Jesus, I receive all that you intend for me to have in the Holy Spirit. I repent of denying the ministry of the Spirit. I repent of mocking believers whose doctrine I did not understand. I repent of valuing tradition over what Your Word teaches.

So now, Father, Abba, I ask. You are the generous Gift-giver. Your heart for me is bigger than the universe. You have a treasure chest filled with gifts for me. So through the powerful presence of Your Holy Spirit, I ask you to deliver and activate those gifts in me.

I pledge to use your gifts for their intended purpose. I pledge to edify—to edify myself so that I may be a stronger disciple and, more importantly, to edify the Body so that it may grow more and more like Your Son, Christ Jesus.

Thank you for your generous and faithful love.

Amen

CHAPTER 3

THE HEALING HEART OF GOD

> *Bless the Lord, O my soul, and forget not all his benefits, who forgives all your iniquity, who heals all your diseases, who redeems your life from the pit, who crowns you with steadfast love and mercy, who satisfies you with good so that your youth is renewed like the eagle's."* (Psalm 103:2–5, ESV)

In February of 2014, I was returning home from a "Church Planter's Conference." We were driving slowly due to the heavy snowfall. With me was my friend, Jerod Long. Jerod and I have been friends since we were toddlers, and we've had about as many life experiences as two friends who happen to be preachers could possibly have. We went to the same schools from kindergarten through college, and played sports on the same teams. We stood in each other's weddings. I married Candace. He married Candice. The Lord touched our hearts in a unique way coming out of college, leading us both to go into lengthy seasons of fasting and prayer in search of a greater understanding of God. We led all-night prayer meetings at my house. While I oversaw academics as Vice President at our Alma Mater, Jerod taught courses in theology at the college and also revolutionized the Bible department at the high school, creating and leading a Biblical Hebrew program. We also co-hosted a weekly radio show, "Theology Without Apology."

When I felt God's call to leave and start a church, Jerod was the first person I asked, and within the week, he received a miraculous confirmation that this was God's plan for us.

Just four weeks out from our church's Grand Opening, battling a snowstorm on our drive home, Jerod received a call from Candice. Their oldest son, Croix, had been found in their home having a severe seizure. Unable to bring him out of it, Candice rushed him to the hospital. So began the lengthy and exhausting journey of caring for a child with severe epilepsy. There was no cure or expected recovery, just a lifetime of medication. As he and Candice adjusted to this new struggle, their other son, Jude, was rushed to the Emergency Room, where doctors discovered a significant mass on his brain. It was a tumor, and it was cancerous. Surgery was scheduled to happen within the week. In one month's time, they'd left home, moved as a family to a new place, and discovered that both of their children had life-threatening illnesses in their brains. As a close friend and pastor to the family, I knew I needed to provide emotional and spiritual support. We hadn't even started our church and had no local church community that could rally around them.

I remember sitting in their home with a bottle of oil in my hand, looking at Jude. He was just two years old, unable to comprehend what he was facing. I poured oil on his head and began to pray. I don't know if I've been as uncertain in prayer as I was at that moment. I felt incompetent as a rookie pastor, guilty that I'd asked my friends to leave the massive network of support that our home church could provide. I felt grief and fear for my dear friends. I felt sad thinking of my two-year-old son, Clarke, Jude's best friend, sitting healthy at my home. Questions flew through my head—one standing out more than all the others. "How do I get Jesus to heal this boy?"

Getting God to heal, according to my understanding at that time, was like winning the lottery. Once in a while, God randomly picks a winner, and they get healed while others are left to suffer or die. I knew that Jesus was filled with compassion while He walked the earth, but I wasn't sure how that translated now that He was in Heaven. I was aware that there was a lot of reference to healing in the Scriptures, but I realized just how little on the topic I knew as I sat there praying. God was merciful. The surgery was a major success. The majority of the tumor was removed, and chemotherapy began. Today, a small portion of the tumor still shows up in scans of Jude's brain, but his health is strong. Jude is a miracle. He and Clarke regularly duke it out on the basketball court and sing worship at the top of their lungs from the second row every Sunday at The Father's House.

The sudden and shocking discovery of these two boys' illnesses shifted something in Jerod and me. Candace and I had our own daily struggles with ongoing childhood illness. Our oldest son, Kenny, has Lamellar Ichthyosis. It's a genetic condition that causes his skin to produce ten times faster than average. He is unable to shed his skin or regulate his body temperature naturally. He is prone to overheating, severe dryness, deep cracks of the skin, and other symptoms depending on the season. While it is not a condition that affects his life span, it certainly affects most other aspects of his life. Treatment of the symptoms is incredibly time-consuming and often quite painful. In 2017, we welcomed our fourth child, Claire, into the world and discovered that she, too, would have to battle this condition.

Healing is a big deal to us. Hundreds of hours spent with doctors and in hospitals, countless prescriptions getting filled, and many long nights filled with tears from both children and parents with passionate prayers offered up to God for help. Healing is a big deal to us.

Thankfully, healing is a big deal to Jesus. A cursory glance through the Gospels reveals that Jesus saw sickness as an enemy. He never excused it, never shrugged his shoulders and said, "Not my problem." He didn't blame His Father for it. Instead, He seemed always to get rid of it. A mom with a fever, a friend who was paralyzed, a beggar who was blind, a woman who couldn't stop bleeding, and a daughter who was severely ill: Jesus healed them all. He healed withered hands, blind eyes, deaf ears, viruses, crippled legs, and skin diseases. Then, in an exciting development, he called His disciples to Himself, laid hands on them, and told them to do the same. The One who healed His friends gave His followers healing power so they could heal *whomever!*

THE EXAMPLE OF JESUS IN THE MINISTRY OF HEALING

What I find strange is that Jesus didn't tell His followers to pray for the sick. He told them to heal the sick. In other words, He said, "Figure out the problem and take care of it." Having watched Jesus, the disciples at least had some visual clues as to what He meant. This is where understanding about the ministry and gifts of healings starts. We need to look at what Jesus did, seeing Him as our Model for perfect obedience to the Father and compassion for the hurting.

In watching Christ's example in the ministry of healing, we see several categories of healing encounters.

- We see people healed because of their faith. "Your faith has made you whole," Jesus said to the woman with the issue of blood. (Luke 8:43-48)
- We see people healed because of their friends' faith. There were four friends who famously tore off the roof of a house to lower their paralyzed friend. (Mark 2:3-11)
- We see people healed because of their persistence. (Luke 18:38-41)

- We see people healed because they were delivered from demons. (See chapter 5 for more on deliverance.) (Luke 13:10-13)

- We see people healed because Jesus wanted to heal them. (John 5:6)

- We see people healed because there was something Jesus wanted them to do. (Luke 4:38-39)

- We see people healed because Jesus wanted them to believe in Him. (John 9:1-7, 35-39)

- We see people healed so that the Father will be glorified. (John 9:1-7)

- We see at least one person that Jesus didn't heal. (Acts 3:1-10)[18]

THE IMPARTATION OF JESUS FOR HEALING MINISTRY

In Luke 9, Jesus calls His disciples to Himself, lays His hands on them, and gives them power to heal the sick. Most believers in the Body of Christ today would not have a problem believing this. Anyone who believes the Bible believes that Jesus had healing power and that His apostles also performed healing miracles. But I think many of us have skipped over Luke 10.

In Luke 10, Jesus seems to destroy the theory of healing only being for Him and the 12 by commissioning 70 others, commanding them to heal the sick. (Luke 10:9)

He gave them His Word, and in obeying it, they walked in His power. Shouldn't this continue with the written Word? Jesus' earthly ministry serves not only as a validation of His identity but also as a demonstration of how His followers should advance the Kingdom. Preach the Kingdom! Cast out, devils! Heal the sick!

---

18 Jesus likely walked by this man often on His way into the Temple.

HEALING IN THE NEW TESTAMENT CHURCH

After the Ascension of Christ, the Apostles continued to demonstrate and teach the ministry of healing. The church's focus was preaching the Gospel, but healing accompanied it. It's clear to me that there were seasons when more people were healed than at other times,[19] but the teaching of the New Testament is also clear that healing is always to be expected and a matter of prayer.

The Scriptures tell us that James was one of the leaders of the church in Jerusalem.[20] Tradition tells us he was a pastor. His epistle gives us great insight into the faith of the early church regarding healing.

Is anyone among you suffering? Let him pray. Is anyone cheerful? Let him sing praise. Is anyone among you sick? Let him call for the elders of the church, and let them pray over him, anointing him with oil in the name of the Lord. And the prayer of faith will save the one who is sick, and the Lord will raise him up. And if he has committed sins, he will be forgiven. Therefore, confess your sins to one another and pray for one another, that you may be healed. The prayer of a righteous person has great power as it is working. Elijah was a man with a nature like ours, and he prayed fervently that it might not rain, and for three years and six months, it did not rain on the earth. Then he prayed again, and heaven gave rain, and the earth bore its fruit. (James 5:13–18)

AN EARLY PASTOR'S PERSPECTIVE

As one who had a front-row seat to the miracles of Jesus, James is quite matter-of-fact about the ministry of healing. He portrays healing as being a grace that is available in the walls of the church. In other words, healing isn't just for the purpose of convincing the lost to get saved, but it is a right for the people of God. His instructions contain no disclaimers and few

---

19 Acts 5:14-16.

20 Acts 15.

qualifications. He essentially says, "If you're sick, tell someone. If the Spirit reveals a sinful cause behind your illness, confess it. Have faith. You'll be healed. We're living in an era where we are all like Elijah, so pray as he did and expect things on a scale like he received." Notice that elders get to pray for healing, but also the "one-anothers" get to pray for healing. Everybody gets to!

If this hasn't been your experience when it comes to dealing with sickness, you're in good company. Most of the church has taken healing and left it between the covers of their Bibles, assuming that the era James lived in is a different one than ours. I believe that the church of Jesus Christ has lost most of what is promised in the Scriptures. It got shelved some time ago, and whoever put it there forgot to tell the next generation where to find it. As King Josiah did as a young King of Judah, there needs to be a generation who cleans out the clutter of tradition and false religion in search of the authentic holiness and power that God has promised. Before Christ's return, I believe levels of healing will return to the church in measures not witnessed since the days of the Apostles.

> *When some people try to tell me that God no longer heals, or that he only heals rarely, I want to ask them, "Where has the Lord's compassion gone? Does Jesus Christ no longer walk among our churches? Does he no longer notice our pain? Does he no longer care for the families who have loved ones in mental hospitals, or whose babies are born with twisted bodies?" I don't think his compassion has changed at all. I think he is just as willing as he was in the first century to touch both our spirits and our bodies. I think it is the church that has changed, not God.*[21]
>
> – Dr. Jack Deere

---

21 Deere, Jack. *Surprised by the Power of the Spirit: Discovering How God Speaks and Heals Today.* Zondervan Academic, Kindle Edition.

HEALING AS A SPIRITUAL GIFT

In I Corinthians 12:9, the Apostle Paul refers to individuals who have been given "gifts of healing by the Spirit." There are within the Body of Christ individuals who have a gift available to them from the Lord to effectively pray for the sick in ways that others cannot. In many churches, singers sing, teachers teach, and servers serve, and little else is allowed. I believe the New Testament perspective is that healing in the church is always available and is as multi-faceted as teaching is. Think with me of all the ways that teaching happens in an average church.

You have the preacher who preaches from the stage at least once per week. You have one-on-one discipleship that takes place. There are classes for children, after-service conversations, small group curriculums, new member classes, and counseling sessions. All of these serve as outlets for the teaching of the Kingdom to occur. With all of this in place, teaching is not limited to just one pastor or gifted teacher. There are dozens of ways that teaching and, conversely, learning can happen. Why can't the ministry of healing be this way? There are sick people in every congregation. Some churches only pray for them from a distance. Others follow part of James 5 and have an elder anoint with oil and pray for healing. However, I see many more options.

- Deliverance ministry done regularly and Biblically should see people healed. As demons flee, they will take their devices of infirmity with them.
- Inner healing ministry, in tandem with deliverance, should also see physical healing.
- Ministry times at the end of public services should result in healing. This is a great place for those gifted with faith and boldness to pray for those who are ill.

- Communion done properly should result in healing. (If doing it poorly results in sickness, I think it's clear that the opposite is also true.)

- Pastoral ministry should result in healing.

- Small group church fellowships should include personal confession and then personal prayer.

- The prophetic ministry should be able to help identify those in the church who have a spiritual gift in this area, as well as help the sick identify in the Spirit reasons why they are ill.

- Evangelism ministry should walk in power evangelism and see converts through the ministry of healing.

Will everyone in the church be healed? Of course not. Will miracles of healing increase in the church exponentially? Yes! God be praised! If this were the perspective on healing that the local church had, then the magnifying of "faith healers" would go away.

BEGINNING TO MINISTER IN HEALING

As I studied this topic while continually praying for Jerod's boys and my own children, I began searching for evidence that God was still healing today. I was stunned at what I found. God is healing people all over the earth. Peer review medical research was being done to verify miraculous healing in response to a believer's prayer.[22] I found scholarly works thousands of pages in length, carefully documenting healing stories around the world.[23] I also had the rich history of my own heritage. While he had never carefully taught how to pray for the sick, my Grandfather certainly had seen many healed.

---

22 *Testing Prayer,* Dr. Candy Gunther Brown. Harvard University Press, 2012.
23 *Miracles: The Credibility of the New Testament Accounts.* Baker Academic, 2011.

I was discussing this all with Jerod one day when his eyes lit up, and he remembered an old family story. His Grandpa Ed had been in construction, and sometime in the 1970s, he had severely injured his back. Doctors recommended surgery and a 6-12 month recovery. Knowing this would leave him unable to provide for his family, Ed's wife drove him to church, where he practically crawled into my Grandfather's office. He anointed Ed with oil and prayed for him. Ed felt nothing until he turned to leave the office. At that point, he says it felt like a board was swung, hitting him in the middle of the back. He fell completely flat on the floor. When he stood up, he was surprised to find that he was completely healed.

Two generations later, Jerod and I continued to seek the Lord's heart for healing. Though we were still not seeing our children healed, we became filled with faith that God wanted to do something significant in our ministries in the area of healing. So, how do you begin healing ministry in your church? You begin praying for the sick.

I started with low-risk ones. My wife, Candace, continually would have severe pain due to TMJ on the left side of her head. Some attacks were so painful that they caused migraines and nausea. One day, as the pain came on, I put my hand on her head and commanded the pain to stop. She kept her eyes closed a second longer before looking at me in shock. "The pain is gone!"

Strangely, it came back the next week, and again, after praying over her a prayer of declaration, it went away. We realized that God was teaching us. The underlying cause of the attacks was still present, but our willingness to take authority over the pain was bringing relief. We had our first lesson: Some healing only deals with the pain.

We continued to persist. One Sunday, a man brought his family to our services. His wife was in a wheelchair. Our old church building has steps everywhere and no ramps or lifts. I helped him carry her up the stairs for the service. I knew this was probably the only time they'd come because we were clearly not equipped for wheelchair access. At the conclusion of the service, I spent some time getting to know them. They were in their mid-30s with a Christian background. She had suddenly lost the ability to walk three years before, and doctors were at a loss. There was no diagnosis and, therefore, no hope for recovery. They told me they hadn't had anyone pray over them but that they would be okay with me anointing them with oil. My faith was at an all-time high, but I was still very new in my understanding. I prayed for them, as did several others in our church. Nothing much happened. They thanked me for the sermon and for praying, and we helped carry her back down the stairs. Surprisingly, they returned for a couple more services, and we prayed for them each time. Within a month of meeting them, doctors discovered a web-like substance on the lower spine that previous scans had not shown. Surgery was scheduled. The substance was removed, and today, the wife walks around as if nothing ever was wrong!

We had our second lesson. God heals in a variety of ways so be obedient to pray and don't lose hope if the result isn't immediate.

Still more opportunities came our way. (There are sick people everywhere that Jesus wants to heal.) A pastor friend called. He'd had a biopsy done and been diagnosed with Stage 4 Lymphoma. I drove down with a friend, and we anointed him with oil and prayed. The next day, we drove him to the hospital. Two weeks later, he called me with the results of the first surgery. They'd removed all of the tissue surrounding the area where they'd done the biopsy. Strangely, none of it showed any cancer. Additional biopsies were done with the same results. The cancer was gone. I learned another lesson. When two people pray for the sick, then neither can claim the credit, and God gets the glory!

Another pastor friend called me. He'd heard that we prayed for the sick, and he was sick! He had a mysterious case of severe acid reflux, ulcers, and insomnia. He told me that as soon as he would lie down to sleep, his chest, throat, and head would start to burn, and then the acid would come up into his throat and begin to choke him. I suspected demons. I brought two friends this time and flew West to see him. He showed me a sleep tracker app on his phone. He hadn't slept more than 4 hours in any night in the last six months. We spent the day with him, praying for him and ministering to his heart. That night, he slept almost 7 hours without pain and woke up without exhaustion. The next night, he slept over 8 hours. When he went to the doctors, they were mystified. Where had all the ulcers and upper respiratory irritation gone?

I learned another lesson. When you minister to the heart of a person with the love of Jesus, He can heal their body.

> *There is one basic reason why Bible-believing Christians do not believe in the miraculous gifts of the Spirit today. It is simply this: they have not seen them. Their tradition, of course, supports their lack of belief, but their tradition would have no chance of success if it were not coupled with their lack of experience of the miraculous. Let me repeat: Christians do not disbelieve in the miraculous gifts of the Spirit because the Scriptures teach these gifts have passed away. Rather they disbelieve in the miraculous gifts of the Spirit because they have not experienced them.*[24] --- Dr. Jack Deere

As passionate as I am about healing and as many times as I've ministered to the sick, I'll still happily admit that I'm still in the kiddie pool of understanding. I still get butterflies when I see someone who needs prayer and try to talk myself out of praying for them.

I've prayed for many people who've not been healed. Others have been healed only to get sick months later. One lady I prayed for was eventually miraculously healed at a revival service that I referred her to of

---

24 Deere, Jack. *Surprised by the Power of the Spirit: Discovering How God Speaks and Heals Today*. Zondervan Academic, Kindle Edition.

cancer in the lungs, only to die two years later from severe lingering effects of COVID-19.

I've learned that praying for anyone for any issue requires boldness, faith, and fresh oil from the Lord. The sick person today won't be healed with the faith that I had for yesterday's miracle. The person in front of me is in desperate need of an encounter with Jesus, and I need to give him a fresh word with fresh power and a heart of love for them. Jesus was able to be in the moment and totally engaged with each person He met. Each person was His creation and a lamb that He deeply loved. May the Spirit help us to minister to individuals with that level of fresh focus and compassion!

THE ABCS OF PRAYING FOR THE SICK

While I'm far from an expert in praying for the sick, I've learned a few things along the way. I wanted to share a process with you to help equip you in this journey of seeing people healed through the power of the Holy Spirit.

I call it "The ABCs of ministering to the sick." They are

1. Ask good questions.
2. Build their faith in Jesus.
3. Cast out any demonic involvement.
4. Determine the correct prayer approach.
5. Encourage the recipient with the next steps to follow.

ASK GOOD QUESTIONS

Don't assume that you know what a person desires prayer for or that they desire prayer at all. Ask if you can pray with them and then patiently and kindly interview them regarding the things about which you can pray. Consider questions like… Would you mind if I prayed with you?

- Is there anything you'd like prayer for?

- Would you be okay if I asked God to heal you?

- Did anything significant happen around the time that this illness/condition began?

The answers you receive to these questions, along with the direction of the Holy Spirit, will help you determine the approach that you will take in prayer.

BUILD THEIR FAITH IN JESUS.

If the person needing prayer is lost, they need the Gospel. Sometimes, Jesus will heal as an impetus for salvation. Other times, their placing of faith in Jesus will bring about healing. Listen to the Spirit.

If the recipient of prayer is already born again, they still need affirmation of the love of Jesus and the kindness of the Father. Many Christians don't believe God wants to heal them. There's a variety of reasons for that. They need to know His love and power are still acting on the earth in healing power. This builds their faith. Never blame them for not having faith. Rather, build up whatever faith they have and encourage them in the Lord. I try to set expectations as I pray for them. I say something like, "Jesus may heal you instantly or gradually. He may heal you miraculously or medically. Regardless, I believe with you that Jesus wants to heal you."

Jesus is the Healer, the Spirit is the Power, and we are the servants.

> *If you want to be used by the Lord in a significant way when you pray for the sick, cultivate a desire to see the Son of God glorified. Wanting only the Son's glory is the most effective way I know to keep ourselves from being deceived and led into error.*[25]
>
> – Dr. Jack Deere

---

25 Deere, Jack. *Surprised by the Power of the Spirit: Discovering How God Speaks and Heals Today.* Zondervan Academic, Kindle Edition.

CAST OUT DEMONIC INVOLVEMENT.

Sometimes, people are sick because demons have been given the right to make them sick. The Holy Spirit typically reveals this during the questions portion. If this is the case. I work through the deliverance process and then pray for their healing.

For more on this, check out chapter 5.

DETERMINE THE CORRECT PRAYER APPROACH.

Sometimes, I ask the Lord in supplication. Other times, I command the pain or disease to go in declaration. Sometimes, I'm not sure and do both. Still, other times, I sense that the Spirit wants the recipient to pray.

ENCOURAGE THE RECIPIENT WITH THE NEXT STEPS TO FOLLOW.

If they are able to test out whether they've been healed or not, then I ask them to do so.

If they have been healed of something that required medical care, I urge them to go to the doctor and get medical verification. I never advise someone to stop taking their medication.

If they haven't seen any improvement, I encourage them to continue seeking prayer, and if they have time, I may work back through some of the previous steps.

It's time for you to go find a person to heal! Let's ask the Lord for help. Pray this aloud.

Father, in the mighty name of Jesus, I ask you to saturate me with a fresh anointing and understanding of your compassionate heart and desire to heal. I confess you are Jehovah Rapha, and I am your child, made in your image, imbued with your power, and filled with your Spirit. Lead me to those in need of your healing touch and fill me with compassion so that I'll love them as you do, wisdom so that I'll speak only what you want me to say, and power so that they may see a demonstration of the Kingdom and desire more of you from it.

Amen

CHAPTER 4

A MEAL WITH JESUS

> *"I am the living bread that came down from Heaven. If anyone eats of this bread, he will live forever. And the bread that I will give for the love of the world is my flesh...Unless you eat the flesh of the Son of Man and drink his blood, you have no life in you. Whoever eats my flesh and drinks my blood has eternal life, and I will raise him up on the last day. For my flesh is true food, and my blood is true drink. Whoever feeds on my flesh and drinks my blood abides in me, and I in him."* From John 6:51-56 (ESV)

I was flying high in the Holy Spirit. It seemed like every time I opened the Scriptures, a new perspective was seen and new insight given to me by the Lord. Candace, though, had hit a little bit of a wall and seemed to be struggling. Despite all that we had been discovering about healing, our oldest son, Kenny, had not been healed, and in October of 2017, we welcomed our 4th child, a precious little girl, Claire. Despite feeling like we were closer to the Lord than we'd ever been before, we were stunned to see that Claire had the same condition. We were both devastated. The ramifications of her having this condition were intense. Our daughter would struggle with pain, her appearance, awkward, time-consuming care, and a life of prescriptions for external and internal treatments. It meant an incredible amount of daily work for my wife. Instead of one being healed, two would suffer.

In this season, I poured myself into reading about communion. It had never been much of a focus for me. It was nothing more than a function of church life, but I felt in my heart that I was missing something of terrible importance. I'd missed out on healing by being ignorant of God's power and Holy Spirit. There had to be something I was missing with communion. This was the last thing Jesus did before His Garden betrayal. It is a unique request and command of our Lord. "Do this in remembrance... often." The Jews of the Old Testament were told to remember, but by forgetting, they wandered into idolatry and lost their freedom. Perhaps the loss of freedom I had experienced in much of my Christian life had something to do with my ignorance concerning this act of remembrance.

It all came to a head one evening after my kids had gone to bed. Candace was angry. Conflict at church was causing us both pain, and our little 7-month-old Claire was having an especially difficult time with her skin. Her skin was dark red, covered in scales and flakes of skin. Her feet had dried and cracked between her toes, and she was bleeding and crying. Candace had bathed her for the second time that day, exfoliated her body, picked through her hair to treat her scalp, and applied lotion to her entire body before putting her in snug pajamas and laying her in her crib. As she came down the stairs, finally finished for the day with this extensive routine, but knowing that tomorrow it would start all over again, her heart broke—not in a weepy way, but in a way that says, "I give up. I'm done. God must not care."

We sat together on the couch, preparing to watch another episode of *The Office*. But spending an empty evening of distraction with some off-color humor to help cope with our pain just didn't seem to be the right thing to do. (The Holy Spirit isn't big on ignoring pain while wasting time with Hollywood).

"Take communion." I felt the Holy Spirit say. "Sit at the table with Candace and talk to Jesus over communion."

"Maybe we should take communion tonight," I said.

My sweet, usually cooperative, meek, and profoundly loving wife looked at me with the most disdainful expression I'd ever seen on her. "I'm good." She said.

Feeling foolish but being driven by a powerful voice in my spirit, I pushed her again. "No, really," I said. "I think it's what we need to do tonight."

So we found our box of Matzos bread in the pantry, poured some grape juice into glasses, and sat at our dining room table. The only problem was I wasn't really sure what to do next. As a pastor, I could walk a crowd of any size through a routine observance of our Lord's Supper without giving it a second thought. But sitting there across the table from just my wife, with the Netflix landing page of a sitcom glowing on our television, I felt foolish. I still remember what I said next. It definitely came from the Holy Spirit.

"What would you say to Jesus if He was sitting here with us right now?" I asked while holding a broken piece of bread in my hand.

Candace's response was the perfect noncommittal Sunday School answer. With little to no expression or passion, she mumbled, "I'd thank him for dying on the cross, I guess."

It was a cliché answer. No gratitude or love was felt in the expression.

So I pushed her. "Really? If Jesus was sitting here right now, that's what you would say?"

Rage appeared on her face. It was one thing to ask her to join me for some spiritual experience. Still, after an incredibly long day of intensive care for a crying infant with difficult needs, I had taken her relaxation time away and then pressured her to talk to Jesus!

She raised her voice at me but yelled at Jesus. "I'd ask Him how could He? How could He do this to our children? Why would He lead us on a journey of discovering His healing power only to afflict our little baby girl and our son? What's wrong with Him?"

I didn't have an answer. Sure, I could point out all of the good things in our lives and the fact that it rains on the just and unjust alike. I could point out the fallen nature of this world and that until the Kingdom was consummated, there would always be sickness. But I knew this wasn't a doctrinal question. This was the cry of a heart that felt abandoned by God.

I don't remember much of our conversation after that. I was more of an eyewitness to something raw, emotional, and deeply moving. Through waves of tears, Candace kept talking to Jesus as if He were sitting in the chair across from her. She broke the bread, sipped the juice, and let Him have it. The more she emptied out the pain of her heart, the more tangible the Presence of Jesus felt in the room. For two hours, she prayed, then I prayed, then we prayed, and then waited on the Lord. Somewhere in that time, the darkness I'd seen in my wife's expression left, and a peace settled over her. She hadn't gotten the answers to her questions, but Jesus had shown up, and though our children weren't healed, we had a Divine assurance that our Father would take care of us.

The following day, with cobwebs in our heads after a very emotional evening, I sat at the kitchen table preparing my sermons for the weekend. Candace came down and told me she was going for a walk to pray. An hour later, she returned to find me still in the same chair, deep in thought.

"Does God often speak out loud to you?" I heard her ask.

"Like out loud out loud?" I replied. "Nope. I've never heard the audible voice of God."

"Oh," she responded, looking overwhelmed.

She went on to tell me that while she'd been on her walk, praying about the events of the previous evening, she'd heard a voice call her name.

"Candace!" She heard, looking around but seeing no one.

"I'm here." The voice said again. "I'm always here."

Tears flowed down her face as she instantly responded. "I know."

Later that day in the evening, our friends Jerod and Candice called us. They'd been trying to teach their sons about the voice of God. Using the story of Samuel, Jerod shared with them the fact that God loves to speak to children. A few minutes after tucking them into bed, Jude, their youngest boy, returned to Jerod. "Dad, I think I just heard God speak to me."

"What did He say?" Jerod said.

"He said, 'I'm here.'"

Candace and I once again wept. What an amazing and validating moment of Divine Harmony! This time, it was tears of joy and worship.

While I have much to say about the ways God speaks to us. The significance of communion in my wife's hearing of God's voice cannot be underestimated. Communion is a physical action that, when obeyed, manifests the spiritual presence of Jesus. In actions of remembrance, we can move into *encounters* with our Lord.

I've come to learn that there are four main views within Christianity concerning communion.

VIEW #1: TRANSUBSTANTIATION – THE CATHOLIC VIEW

Catholicism teaches that as the participant takes the bread and wine, the elements become the very flesh and blood of Christ.

Wayne Grudem writes, "Transubstantiation According to the teaching of the Roman Catholic Church, the bread and wine actually become the body and blood of Christ. This happens at the moment the priest says, "This is my body" during the celebration of the Mass. At the same time as the priest says this, the bread is raised up (elevated) and adored. This action of elevating the bread and pronouncing it to be Christ's body can only be performed by a priest."

Grudem continues, "The Catechism of the Catholic Church teaches the following: In the most blessed sacrament of the Eucharist, "the body and blood, together with the soul and divinity, of our Lord Jesus Christ and, therefore, the whole Christ is truly, really, and substantially contained."[26]

VIEW #2: CONSUBSTANTIATION – THE LUTHERAN VIEW

The original Protestant, Martin Luther, originally a Catholic priest himself, discovered dozens of areas in faith and practice where he saw the teaching of the Catholic Church as being in direct opposition with the content of the Scripture. Communion was one such area. Luther saw that the atoning work of Christ was finished, yet the phrase "this is my body" that Jesus used still needed to be taken in some literal sense. Grudem writes, "He (Luther) concluded not that the bread actually becomes the physical body of Christ but that the physical body of Christ is present "in, with, and under" the bread of the Lord's Supper."[27]

VIEW #3: REAL PRESENCE – THE VIEW OF THE REFORMERS

The Reformers who picked up where Luther left off and moved further away from Catholicism found that Luther stopped a little too short in his departure from transubstantiation. They found that he still took too literal an approach to the presence of body and blood somehow being in the elements. The Reformers affirmed that the presence of Christ was a certainty

---

26 Grudem, Wayne. *Systematic Theology*, Second Edition (p. 1223-1224). Zondervan Academic.,Kindle Edition.

27 Grudem, Wayne. *Systematic Theology*, Second Edition (p. 1227). Zondervan Academic, Kindle Edition.

during communion but *only* in a spiritual sense and not at all in a physical sense.

VIEW #4: MEMORIALISM – THE VIEW OF BAPTISTS

In my understanding, the majority of Baptists observe communion purely as an act of remembrance. There is little expectation of the Lord's Presence, so little to no spiritual experience is had. There may be some emotion that comes out of love for the One who gave Himself for us, but there is typically no time taken to look for or revel in the Real Presence of Christ.

Wherever you find a Catholic, you'll find a Baptist on the opposite end of the spectrum. While this is Scripturally defensible in many cases, I have discovered that in other cases, it is a position rooted in fear or in a misguided thought process that everything the Catholic Church does is unscriptural. I believe this has become the case with the Baptist view of communion. I believe that in my Baptist upbringing, I missed out on the vast majority of the power of communion. Don't get me wrong, in my home church, communion was quite an event. With somewhere around 4,000 people assembled in one room, feeding them all in a timely manner took some thought. We had communion, or as it was most often called "Lord's Supper," about once per month. To be perfectly honest, I did not look forward to it. I wanted to get home and watch my Chicago Bears play. Lord's Supper usually meant that the service would go longer than usual and that we would hear a second sermon—one to introduce communion and another during the normal message time slot. As many as 150 ushers and deacons would line up across the stage and receive gleaming silver platters specially made to hold dozens of tiny wafers or dozens of tiny plastic cups filled with grape juice. (Remember: We were Baptists. Wine would not be tolerated.). The game I played with any friend sitting with me was finding an uncut "double" wafer, which made the event a touch more exciting. You're probably thinking I was a cynical, heartless, damaged preacher's kid, and you're probably right. But cynicism aside, discoveries and experiences I've had in recent years of taking communion have opened my eyes to the fact that communion is more than a tradition done for the sake of a memorial.

Cemeteries are filled with memorials. There are tombs, headstones, benches bearing engraved name plates, and mausoleums with images and names, all in remembrance of the dead. Remembering the dead has its place, but we serve the God of the living, the Creator who through His Resurrected Son gives eternal life! Ironically, a significant problem that Baptists have with crucifixes is that they portray a dying Savior still attached to His cross, yet when it comes to communion, their approach is in a similar vein. They tend to remember Him in such a way that one would feel as if He is still in the grave. The Scriptures are clear. Communion is all about the death of Christ. When we take communion, we proclaim His death, but as we proclaim His death, we should expect His living presence to join us. When we proclaim His death, He comes and reminds us that He is very much alive. There is a blessing that comes with taking communion, even if just as a memorial because it is an action of obedience and Gospel proclamation. Still, I've come to see and believe the Scriptures promise that there is considerably more, specifically in the areas of healing, presence, power, and fellowship.

HEALING FOUND IN COMMUNION

Physical and spiritual healing is a topic much larger than in just the context of spiritual gifts. The New Testament has a level of expectation and certainty in regard to healing that most Christians just simply do not have today. Jesus told His followers to "heal the sick." Pastor James of the Church in Jerusalem said in his letter, "The prayer of faith will save the sick." Mark concludes his Gospel account by stating that followers of Jesus will "lay hands on the sick, and they will recover." As I've written elsewhere, understanding healing requires a person to understand the effects of sin's curse, the doctrine of suffering, the compassion of Jesus, the influence of demons, the necessity of faith, and finally, the power of communion. Communion taken poorly makes people sick and, in some extreme cases, causes death! (I Corinthians 11:27-31) Isn't it then logical to see that communion taken correctly preserves the healthy, gives healing to the sick, and could possibly even raise a person from their deathbed? If the presence of Jesus, as seen in the Gospels, often resulted in healing and resurrection, then should we expect less when His very Spirit lives inside us?

THE PROMISE OF PRESENCE IN COMMUNION

As you read the Bible, you'll find that there aren't many actions where presence is explicitly promised. This is one reason why communion is such a precious gift. You are allowed to take it as often as you like. As long as you follow the instructions of Scripture, you can be sure that Jesus is with you in it. Yes, the Scriptures promise us that Jesus is always with us and won't ever leave us, but communion takes it further. It is an act that brings Him closer to our awareness. I so long to be closer to Jesus! Communion has done this for me on so many occasions. The fact that three of the four major views on Communion within the Body of Christ believe that there is a real Presence of Jesus in this ordinance should not be ignored.

THE FRUITFULNESS THAT COMES FROM IMPLANTING THE BODY

Many of my Baptist friends may find this point to be the strangest of my communion points. Bear with me. I believe that Jesus was purposely offensive and direct in His statements on communion to expose the hearts of the Pharisees; but I think it's also likely that His direct statements of "eat my flesh and…drink my blood" have additional significant meaning. We know from science and nutritionists that what we eat has a direct effect on how we feel and our long-term health. The food we eat is a seed that will bear fruit in our future health. Toxic food will produce sickly health. Healthy food, we expect, would produce vibrant health. Taking time to carefully observe communion while believing that the metaphor of the bread and juice still has powerful connections to Christ's Body and Blood leads us to long-term fruitfulness. The elements of communion are the seeds of faith that, when planted in our souls, bear much fruit for the Kingdom of Heaven. How this occurs is undoubtedly a mystery. So is the gift of tongues, the ministry of prophecy, and the indwelling of the Holy Spirit. If I invite the Presence of Christ into my body regularly, shouldn't I expect a long-term fruitfulness in my Christian walk? Lastly, we know that eating one healthy meal doesn't guarantee us long-term health. It is a steady diet of healthy foods that produces results. Continued participation in communion has a gradual but steady effect—it makes us more and more like Jesus.

THE POWER OF THE BLOOD FOUND IN COMMUNION

I don't know of any substance more precious or powerful than the blood of Jesus. Preceding the Exodus, the sight of lamb's blood on the doorpost spared the lives of countless Jewish children before they exited Egypt. Still today, the practice of pleading and applying the blood of Christ in prayer and declaration is a mighty act that cancels the plans of demons and causes the enemy to go somewhere else with his plans of destruction. I believe that the act of communion opens our lives up to greater access to the power of Christ's blood. When I take communion, I am not just claiming the blood in a general sense but also bringing its power into my body. No, I do not believe that the juice I drink in communion becomes the blood. Instead, I think the physical act of taking communion produces a potent spiritual result. If our lack of prayer prevents God from answering, then I believe the principle applies that a lack of participation with Him in communion limits the extent to which His blood has active power in our lives.

As I strongly urge you to make communion a greater part of your walk with the Lord, I trust that you will not misinterpret my passion for it. Communion is not a good luck charm, nor is it a substitute for the other valuable disciplines of a believer's life. It is also not to be trifled with.

Bitterness, sexual perversion, and other unconfessed sins can create severe issues, including illness. It is an act of power. Done correctly, we should believe that it aligns us with God's purposes and fills us with His power. Done flippantly, we should be concerned about the effects of "playing with the power of God."

Are you ready to make communion a part of your life? Perhaps you're in a crisis, and you desperately need to raise a glass of juice in the air and plead the blood of Jesus over the situation. I urge you to do it.

INSTRUCTIONS

When I take communion at home, I do so in three different contexts.

I occasionally observe it with my family. This is a joyful time around the dinner table, as we invite Jesus to join us. Each member of the family is challenged with a theme or topic to share with Jesus while the rest of us listen in. These are special times as long as I don't take myself too seriously and don't put any pressure on my kids to be anything more than simple in their faith.

I also observe communion with just one other person. This is most often my wife, but there are times when, as a pastor or mentor, I've sat down with someone and led them through this meal to encourage them in the presence of Jesus.

Lastly, I regularly take communion alone. I see myself sitting with Jesus, and so I take my time working through the elements of the meal. This is a time for worship, gratitude, and then listening.

The example Jesus sets for us in communion is one of participation with His followers. Our observance at home should never be done in place of regular observance with a local Body. The first communion was held in the midst of puffed-up apostles, each jockeying for position on the corporate ladder of the Kingdom. The presence of Jesus kneeling before them and washing their feet put an end to all of that. If you've gotten away from church because you've seen the ugly side, I encourage you to look again.

Consider these words from my prayer journal in 2020.

Jesus' church is beautiful. Scandals, failures, manipulations, heresies, and cheap imitations may have caused you to leave a place you called "church." You may have promised yourself you'd never go back. Rest assured, Jesus hasn't left you, nor does He wish for you to remain separated from an assembled branch of His Body. There is a place for you. Keep praying, keep seeking, keep searching, and when you find the place He has for you, keep going.

You'll see the beauty of the Body again.

You'll feel the love of Jesus through the saints.

You'll see that the Church of Jesus is advancing and winning.

Jesus has forgiveness for you. Don't let bitterness destroy you.

Jesus has healing for you. Don't let your wounds define you.

Jesus has a place for you. Don't let loneliness restrain you.

Don't give up. A new view of the beauty of Jesus is just around the corner.

A PRAYER FOR COMMUNION

(Begin to use this prayer before communion in order to prepare your heart for encounter.)

Father, in the name of Jesus, I ask that you renew my understanding of enjoying the presence of Jesus through the power of communion. Teach me about His death, that I might learn to die well. Teach me about the blood, that I might live under its holy power. Teach me about your heart, that I might burn brighter with its glorious compassion.

Show me His Beauty: The wounded Healer who lives forevermore. All blessing, and honor, and glory be unto You!

Amen

CHAPTER 5

CASTING OUT DEVILS

> *And Jesus went away from there and withdrew to the district of Tyre and Sidon. And behold, a Canaanite woman from that region came out and was crying, "Have mercy on me, O Lord, Son of David; my daughter is severely oppressed by a demon." But he did not answer her a word. And his disciples came and begged him, saying, "Send her away, for she is crying out after us." He answered, "I was sent only to the lost sheep of the house of Israel." But she came and knelt before him, saying, "Lord, help me." And he answered, "It is not right to take the children's bread and throw it to the dogs." She said, "Yes, Lord, yet even the dogs eat the crumbs that fall from their master's table." Then Jesus answered her, "O woman, great is your faith! Be it done for you as you desire." And her daughter was healed instantly.* (Matthew 15:21–28, ESV)

I was out of town with family for vacation when a former student from my days teaching at Bible College called. He was in his 30s, happily married, and entering his second decade of full-time ministry. There was one significant problem. He was being attacked by a demon. Here's his account:

In January of 2023, I attended a preaching conference where I heard a sermon that encouraged me to take a major step in pursuing God. That night, I was awoken to sleep paralysis by a figure robed in white moving rapidly around the bed where I was sleeping. I was held down by a pressure that covered me totally. I couldn't lift a finger, move a limb, or even speak. After probably thirty to sixty seconds, I was finally released and was able to sit up in my bed. Fully awake, I was convinced what I had experienced was both real and was not the first time it had happened.

Nearly twenty years earlier, when I was only twelve, my Mom had experienced an evil spiritual presence three separate times, which woke her from her sleep. The first two times, she had "prayed it away," but the third time, she confronted it and told the spirit, "I belong to Jesus. You can't have me." The demon pushed her down and held her for a moment before leaving. She later discovered my father's pornography and is certain the presence was tied to that. In fear, she spoke with me the following day, warning me of the presence that was in the house. That night, I was visited by a demon and held down in my sleep for the first time. When I was eventually released from the "sleep paralysis," I sat up and decided that I must have dreamed the experience due to going to bed scared of demons. I decided not to tell my mom since she had been so scared the day before, and I was regularly visited by demons from that point forward. I often encountered evil spiritual presences just in regular life, often making me scared of dark places, like the basement, the garage, and other unfamiliar locations like a store, a library, etc. I was awoken to sleep paralysis for the following 18 years at least monthly, with seasons of time where it was more or less regular; each time, I assumed, "I must have been thinking about demons last night, which is why I dreamed about them." The devil is subtle and a master of deceit; he will trick you and let you believe anything that furthers his work.

As memories of specific demonic encounters started flooding back into my mind, I started the work of finding answers. I listened to sermons and bought books on spiritual warfare. I spoke with my wife and told her for the first time what had happened and my ability to regularly sense the presence of *spirits. I called both of my (now divorced) parents seeking more information and found none. I spoke with four pastors looking for answers, getting prayer from some, only one of which had any answers, but none of the answers brought relief. I was told by one that "you may be like Paul, having a thorn in the flesh, and God just wants you to have it." As the days progressed, the spiritual warfare became heavily increased. What started off as a singular show of power to someone who desired to pursue God became regular and unending torment. As I learned and grew in my walk with God, the demons dropped the gloves and started attacking me twice a week, then three times, then more.*

In March, my wife left for a quick trip to visit family, leaving me on vacation at home with my kids. Every night she was gone, I was visited starting at about midnight through five a.m. The spirits would come to our bedroom and cause me back pain and dizziness. They even twisted my arm unnaturally if I tried to command them to leave in Jesus' name. I was defenseless to their attacks. I would sit awake every night that week, reading my Bible, praying, and crying as my young children whimpered in their beds a few feet away. After not sleeping for days and feeling miserable, my wife asked me if I had considered contacting Ken. I reached out via Facebook. I told him that I had been experiencing some spiritual warfare and would appreciate any help he could give. He agreed to call me in an hour.

When Ken called, and I had explained my story, he instantly diagnosed the origin of the demonization from my conversation with my mom, something none of the other pastors had been able to do. She had unintentionally given permission for the spirits to approach me, saying something like, "This could happen to you, so if it does, tell me." Authority given, the spirits then had free rein in my life. He then explained there are several strongholds Satan will use to gain access to your life: bitterness, sexual sin, idolatry, witchcraft, and generational iniquities. He recommended I take some time and pray through the first four, asking the Holy Spirit to show me anything from which I needed to repent or forsake. Next, he told me to bring a spiritually strong friend over (since my wife was out of town) and anoint my home with oil, binding the demons. Then, he prayed over me, taking authority in Jesus' name and binding the spirits from me. We also planned a meeting via Zoom about two weeks later to deal with all the residual demonization I couldn't get deliverance from alone. I followed his directions of confession and anointing, and the demonic presence in my home was instantly reduced from 100% to 20%. The battle was not over; they still had legal right to stay, but they no longer had power over me. I could sense their continued presence, but they no longer hurt me or woke me up with sleep paralysis.

When my day of deliverance finally arrived, we sat down for a three-hour Zoom meeting where I confessed things that had a hold over me (James 5:16) and was awestruck as the Holy Spirit led their team through the steps to help me find healing and freedom. God had miraculously provided at least four separate words of knowledge that gave me confidence in the process I was embarking on. Several times through the process, I could feel the spirits "pushing" or putting pressure on me to cause fear and disrupt our work. They caused shaking and discomfort throughout the deliverance session. Ken ended each attempt to distract me by simply commanding them to stop in Jesus' name. Ken's team led me to experience the love of Christ for myself and then broke generational curses and helped me break all ties to demonic forces one by one. We delivered the demons to Jesus, and I finally experienced the peace that passes all understanding. Ken warned of evil spirits seeking to return (Luke 11:24-26), encouraging me to fill my house, build up my defenses, and seek to deepen my relationship with Father God.

Since I received deliverance in April, I have not experienced any more sleep paralysis. I have experienced spiritual attacks where a demon sought to regain entrance into my life, but all attacks have been defeated by the power of Jesus Christ and through the blood He shed on Calvary. It is, however, worth noting that God's gift of discerning of spirits has continued in my life. I still sense evil spirits—even ones that aren't specifically attacking me. I sense them with others. I walk into empty rooms and can feel their presence and have even held inconspicuous inanimate objects that retained some level of demonic attachment. The difference now is three-fold: I no longer fear what I experience, evil spirits no longer take up residence in our home, and demons no longer have power over me. Through my gifting, I am able to "war a good warfare" and defend against the spiritual attacks from the enemy by the power of Jesus Christ and the defense system of the armor of God (Ephesians 6), and God has further equipped me to begin doing deliverance ministry as He has called me to "break the chains for His children."

One of the most effective lies that the Devil ever sold the church was that demons don't take control of Christians. Like many areas of Christian doctrine, there is a split over terminology and tradition in the area of demonic influence, causing a large percentage of the Body of Christ not to believe that demons can interfere in their lives at all.

The testimony above is from one of many individuals I've prayed with who have testimonies of being born again and significant fruit in their lives that validates their faith. Still, they are under significant torment from demons. Their spiritual leaders insist that they can't be demon-possessed, and therefore are of little help, totally ignorant to the simple truth that the majority of their congregations enter their church sanctuary each Sunday with demons attached to them!

Everywhere Jesus went, demons manifested. His power exposed their fear. His love exposed their hatred. His holiness exposed their evil. His peace exposed their destructive natures. His obedience to the Father exposed their anarchy. The presence of Jesus exposes demons. As I grew in my understanding of this, I became very concerned about my church. If no demons were manifesting, might it mean that the powerful presence of Jesus wasn't there?

Truthfully, in many churches, demons do manifest, but the church has learned secular ways of labeling and dealing with them. Addicts to pornography get accountability partners and special web-browsing soft-ware.[28] Divisive people are given a personality test so that people will know how to better avoid pushing their buttons. Depressed people get meds.

---

28 These things have their place in the Body after deliverance has occurred.

Substance abusers get 10 steps or their own Friday night discipleship program. Everyone else gets counseling. Few get lasting freedom.

I battled pornography consistently for over 20 years. Then Jesus dropped His Spirit on me while I painted a basement bathroom, and everything changed. I learned afterward that what I thought was the flesh was actually a demonic power taking over parts of my life and controlling me. Most of the Church doesn't realize there is a difference between temptation and "triggers." Nearly all triggers are heart wounds that are infected by demons. When the demons were removed, and the wounds began to heal, the desire and temptation concerning pornography withered up and died. Do I still experience temptation? Of course, but the pressure is external, and I am presented with a choice. In contrast, when I had infected heart wounds, I could be triggered and feel like I had no choice, controlled by some dark force. God makes a way out of temptation (I Corinthians 10:13), and the first step in discovering that way is to experience deliverance and inner healing.

Since God set me free, I have seen dozens of people set free from the addictions they had to perversion and immorality. I don't preach against perversion nearly as much as I used to. Instead, I pray with the shamed, the confused, and the misidentified and watch God set them free. While I know it's important to confront the sin of the unrepentant, I've found that most people are scared that they can't stop doing the things they know are wrong. They are willing to open up and be honest with someone who will love them and get them to Jesus for freedom.

THE MATTER OF CONTROL

Deliverance ministry is a counterattack against the advances made by Satan and his demons. The Cross and Resurrection broke the back of the enemy and subdued every power under the authority of Jesus. However, in Satan's final stand, warfare continues as the world and many Christians go through life without an understanding of what the Cross has done for them. The enemy's plan is simple. He wants to take control. If he has control, he can do what he wants: lie, blaspheme, steal, kill, and destroy. Enemy control looks like a person who has a troubled area in their life. It looks like a person who can't ever get ahead. It looks like bad habits, troubled relationships, and sometimes chronic illness. The enemy takes control through distraction, deception, division, domination, and destruction.

DISTRACTION

I believe that distraction is the most prevalent form of temptation in the modern world. Some are distracted to avoid their past, others because they're blind to the possibilities of their potential. Most of us are completely unaware of God's vision for us because we are continually engrossed in the visions of the world. Not to be cheesy, but it's literally in the word *television*. We watch too much, scroll too much, and play too much. We work hard, which is honorable, except for the problem of what it is that we are working *for*. Many of us don't have time for the Lord because we are so busy trying to keep up or get ahead in order to obtain. Apparently, this isn't just an American problem. James said to the church in Jerusalem that we pervert prayer because we ask for things that we will just consume with our lusts.[29] Two of the fruits of the Spirit that I think Paul forgot to mention were the fruits of focus and clarity. Okay, they're probably by-products of peace and the other eight,[30] but you get my point. In Ephesians chapter 1, Paul prayed that the eyes of our hearts would be enlightened. This is a prayer for spiritual sight. Jesus told the seven churches in Revelation to listen to what the Spirit is saying. This is a plea for spiritual hearing. The enemy's plan is to blind and deafen us to the work of the Spirit, and one way he accomplishes this is through distraction.

---

29 James 4:1-3.

30 See Galatians 5:22-23.

It's amazing how when the Holy Spirit falls on someone, all of the time wasters and coping mechanisms that they had seem to wither away. I'm embarrassed at how much time I wasted in entertainment before the Spirit fell on me. Suddenly, the sitcoms weren't that funny, the dramas felt dark and pointless, and the action seemed ridiculous.

On the other hand, I found myself desperately hungry for new adventures in the Holy Spirit and the next whisper of God's voice. The enemy is super-effective at distracting us. For the sheep, he distracts with ignorance, but when someone breaks through that ignorance, he just pushes them into paranoia. Many conspiracy theorists discovered the truth only to go to the other extreme and become paranoid.

DECEPTION

Satan takes what distracts us and creates a lie around it. The lie that we need it, or the lie that it will make us happier, along with a thousand others. He's the "father of lies."[31] He tells a lot of them, and he's very good at getting us to believe them. Each lie we believe gives Satan a measure of control in our lives. The only way to counteract the onslaught of deception that comes against a believer is to be grounded in the Word of God and filled with the Spirit of Truth. The Spirit of Truth, which is the Holy Spirit, keeps the Word fresh in our souls, selecting the passages we need for each situation we face. The Word helps us discern the difference between the voice of the Spirit and the voices of other spirits. To walk in the Spirit and not fulfill the lusts of the flesh and avoid being deceived by the enemy, we must have two legs. One step is in the Spirit, and the next is in the Word. A Word-and-Spirit lifestyle is the only way to walk with God and remain in truth.

One effective way that Satan deceives believers is by substituting tradition in place of the Word. Many use the Word to support their traditions. In extreme cases, people go to the extreme of changing the Word to support

---

31 John 8:44.

their beliefs. This demonic tactic goes all the way back to the serpent in the Garden. Questioning and critiquing the Word brings deception.

With the tools of distraction and deception, the enemy has created a counterfeit of walking in the Spirit. Instead of Word and Spirit, Satan provides lies and imaginations. *For though we walk in the flesh, we do not war after the flesh: For the weapons of our warfare are not carnal, but mighty through God to the pulling down of strongholds; casting down imaginations, and every high thing that exalteth itself against the knowledge of God, and bringing into captivity every thought to the obedience of Christ.* (2 Corinthians 10:3–5, KJV)

Lies are Satan's version of truth. Imaginations are Satan's version of Spirit. Imaginations are thought processes or philosophies whispered by the spirits of darkness into the hearts of humanity. Satan sells a lie, then builds a thought process and set of behaviors around it. In the Garden of Eden, the serpent told Eve, "When you eat the fruits, you shall not die."[32]

Once she had a lie from the serpent to build on, she saw the fruit differently. She now had a thought process that led to disobedience. Eve heard and saw. It's that simple. If you hear and see in Word and Truth, you will live in freedom. If you hear and see in error and deception, you will live in bondage.

DIVISION

Satan creates lies that contradict each other, and then he rallies separate individuals or groups behind both lies. Sometimes, both sides of the coin are wrong because Satan is the one who minted the coin in the first place. In our personal lives, Satan uses the lies we believe to separate us from others. Even if we are around people all day, we can still feel separated from them because of what is in our hearts. Satan loves to isolate people so that he can bully them. The primary message of Jesus to His disciples before His

---

32 Genesis 3:1-6.

death was that they would love one another and walk in unity. Ever since, the church has struggled with conflict and strife. A clear sign of demonic interference in a person's life is apathy towards unresolved conflict.

In some cases, reconciliation is impossible. However, in many cases, people walk through life in bitterness and resentment, ignorant of the demonic attachments that have been made in their lives. The Bible cautions us to be vigilant in God's grace, lest a root of bitterness spring up and defile us.[33] The fruit of failing to forgive is demonic control. More on this in Chapter 8.

The parable of the wheat and the weeds[34] gives us great insight into this matter of division. Because the enemy cannot destroy the wheat of God's Word,[35] he has sown many weeds. Discerning God's voice among this world's thousands of opinions and objections is as challenging as ever. May God help us walk in a spirit of truth and unity!

DOMINATION

When you have believed enough of his lies and have been separated physically or emotionally from community, Satan begins to force himself on you with torment and anguish. You may or may not recognize it as being from Satan, but you know deep down that something is terribly wrong. You are no longer in control of your own life, even though all the bills and responsibilities have your name on them. There are powers at work that seem to be way ahead of you all of the time. You are now a slave and must helplessly watch as the enemy begins to pick at the people around you whom you love the most. Consider the story of Lot. When division arose between his servants and his Uncle Abram's servants, they were forced to part ways. Distracted by the lush nature of the valley, Lot moved towards

---

33 Hebrews 12:15.

34 Matthew 13:24-30.

35 Matthew 24:35.

Sodom.[36] Deception drew him from being a herdsman outside the city into being a judge in the city. Now, he was separated by boundary and culture from Abram's protection. It wasn't long before he was caught up in a battle between nine kings, and he, along with his family, was taken as spoils of war. The decision Lot made to move to Sodom resulted in putting his whole family into captivity. In spite of being rescued by his uncle's army of servants,[37] the enemy's domination of Lot would continue, causing most of his family to perish in God's judgment of Sodom.[38]

DESTRUCTION

We are made in the image of God. Satan takes great delight in destroying anything that looks like God. Satan is not just looking to kill us but to cause as much collateral damage as possible. He wants to destroy hope for an entire generation.

Thank God the enemy's plan will fail.

No matter how bleak these steps of Satanic invasion may look, there is a solution for each one of them. The Word of God exposes distraction. The Spirit of God sheds light on deception. God's love and peace heal division. God's Kingdom power rescues those under domination in Satan's bondage. God's healing and restoration power can undue Satan's attempts at destruction.

Maybe you see yourself in the grip of the enemy. Maybe you can already look back at the ways that lies you've believed have produced toxic fruits that have destroyed relationships and led friends and family captive. God can deliver you and restore what the enemy has taken. Deliverance is the children's bread. One of the earliest pictures of this is in the story of Lot. The name "Abram" means "exalted father." The exalted Father loves to

---

36 Genesis 13:7-13.

37 Genesis 14.

38 Genesis 19.

rescue his adopted children and bring them to Jesus. That's what He's done for me. It's what He'll do for you.

THE CHURCH'S RELATIONSHIP WITH DELIVERANCE

If you haven't figured it out yet, I believe it's clear that the church has a demon problem. Some are fighting over terms like "possession" and "oppression." A spirit of religion and division is at work.

Others are so worldly that they're embarrassed by any Christian brothers and sisters who still would be so superstitious and archaic as to believe in demons. After all, we have modern medicine now. Science has revealed to us the real causes of these issues. A spirit of humanism is at work.

Still other parts of the church have made deliverance ministry a circus. Demons get more attention than Jesus. They know the names of all the characters of darkness but lack Biblical wisdom, Gospel preaching, and understanding of the church. A spirit of confusion is at work.

I haven't figured out everything there is to know about the Kingdom of Darkness, nor do I want to, and I certainly don't expect everyone to handle deliverance the exact same way I do. Still, God has given me and my ministry partners incredible favor in the ministry of deliverance, and I believe the Lord wants me to share some insight.

DELIVERANCE IS PART OF THE GOSPEL AND REQUIRES THE GOSPEL

Whenever Jesus preached the Gospel of the Kingdom or instructed His followers in their preaching ministries, He included healing and deliverance. The preaching of the Kingdom confronts demons. The Kingdom advances through proclamation, and each advance pushes demons back, ultimately causing them to reveal themselves and fight back. We fight with the Word of truth. They fight back with words of intimidation and accusation. We have the spirit of power, love, and self-control. They have the spirit of fear.

Nearly every week of my life, I share the Gospel with a follower of Jesus who needs deliverance. These are individuals who are already saved but who have been blinded to some part of the Gospel by a lie from the enemy. The lies are not complex or very creative:

"God doesn't love you."

"You are a disappointment to God."

"You are a failure, and everyone is about to find out."

"You haven't done nearly enough to earn God's favor."

After identifying some of the ways that Satan has bound them, I begin to remind the person I'm working with of some of the key truths of the Gospel.

"The Cross was enough."

"The Resurrection took all of Satan's power."

"Jesus has all authority."

"You really are a child of God."

Once the truth of the Gospel has sunk in, I can begin to expose the lies the enemy has told. As lies are exposed, demons lose their rights. When their rights to torment are canceled, demons leave with a simple word. The Gospel is the light that makes the darkness flee.

As you read this, you may think it sounds too simple. I have two responses. First, Jesus is really simple. He's really powerful, infinitely brilliant, and unconditional in His love, but He is simple. John 3:16 isn't complicated. Faith is child-like. Don't let all the drama that surrounds deliverance in the church world cause you to overcomplicate things.

Second, I think you would be amazed at how many pastors I talk to who don't believe God loves them. Over the past few years, I've had frank conversations with dozens of pastors. Well over 70% of them have admitted to me that they struggle with believing that God loves them. If that's what the leaders believe, what does the average person in the pew believe?

This issue of deliverance is not about all that we can learn about demons, darkness, and their many devices. You don't always need to know their names. You don't need to memorize the latest 10-step process to send demons running. All that stuff can help on occasion. But at its core, deliverance is about a simple Jesus and His love for people. The magic words in deliverance ministry are most often, "God loves you."

> *The argument has also been made that if we are full of the Holy Spirit then we can't have a demon in us. I agree with that. I just don't believe that most Christians are full of the Holy Spirit—or remain full at all times. We can be full of the Holy Spirit and have something happen to us that causes us to respond in an unbiblical way. When we do that, we set ourselves up, creating an opening for affliction. We need to develop the spiritual habit of a biblical response to the trials of life so that the enemy cannot find any opening through which he can bring affliction.*[39]
>
> – Dr. Randy Clark

THE GOSPEL OF THE KINGDOM VERSUS THE GOSPEL OF REPENTANCE

One reason many Gospel-preaching churches do not encounter many demons is that they do not preach the Gospel of the Kingdom. During his ministry, John the Baptist preached the Lamb, who would take away the sins of the world. He made disciples. He baptized people. His message outlasted his lifetime by decades. However, the Scriptures never show him casting out a demon. Today, many churches have taken John's message and

---

39 Clark, Randy. *The Biblical Guidebook to Deliverance* (pp. 51-52). Charisma House, Kindle Edition.

simply changed the tense. John preached a Jesus who would come to earth. They preach a Jesus who once came to earth.[40]

The Gospel of the Kingdom preaches the Cross and the Second Coming, but it also preaches the present-tense King. Once you begin to preach the Kingdom that is here now and overtaking the darkness, demons will manifest. Why? Because the preaching of the Kingdom reveals (or manifests) the Kingdom and exposes the enemy.

DELIVERANCE IS A MINISTRY OF, IN, AND FROM THE LOCAL CHURCH

If deliverance is a part of the Gospel, then every part of the church should work together to incorporate the message of freedom in their process. Ideally, all parts of the local church work together in deliverance internally to minister to the Body and externally as a work of outreach for the lost. Over the last several years, I've run into dozens of ministries completely disconnected from any local church that offer deliverance, prayer, and inner healing. While a few work to maintain relationships with pastors for accountability, many are outside the church because they've been hurt in the past. Essentially, they are providing a service of healing and deliverance while they themselves need healing from their wounds and reconciliation with the Body of Christ. I am wary of these ministries. While their treatments may bring relief in the short term, they often fail to provide long-term healing and strengthening for their clients because they don't have a covering or connection with a church or network of churches. I'm for anyone who preaches Jesus and helps people find freedom. However, I'm a passionate defender of the local church. We need them in this hour as much as at any time since Pentecost. Deliverance ministry done in the midst of a community of believers who are established as a local church should be the norm.

---

40 To be fair, some do preach the Second Coming as well, but they have little present sense of the Kingdom.

The authority structure for deliverance ministry is pretty simple within the confines of a local church. When the leadership establishes a culture of healthy freedom ministry, demons get uncomfortable. A Body of believers in unity against the powers of darkness is beautiful.

THE IMPORTANCE OF AUTHORITY

With your message (Gospel of the Kingdom) and your mode (Local Church) in order, you can begin to effectively and safely deal with the enemy. Demons understand authority and recognize faith. Demons don't respond to volume or physical force. They aren't threatened by displays of Bible knowledge or Scripture quotations. They respond to authority. Even a child confident in the authority found in being a son or daughter of the King can cast out a demon.

When Adam and Eve sinned in the Garden, they gave away their dominion and authority over the earth. When Jesus cried, *"Tetelestai"* on the Cross, He declared Satan's rule as finished. When He walked out of the Garden Tomb, He proved it. He now possessed the "keys of the Kingdom" and has been willing to share them with His followers ever since. Deliverance is a ministry of eviction. In real estate, evictions must be done according to the Law. A judge sends an authorized and empowered officer to carry out the eviction. The Scriptures are the eviction notice, but still, an officer with an understanding of his role is needed to empty the house of the squatters. Most evictions are not physically violent. There may be an exchange of unpleasant words, but the orders stand, and the house is emptied. Deliverance ministry is the same. The demons will make threats, complain about the conditions, and mock everyone involved, but they've been on notice for 2,000 years. They know they have to go. Once in a while, they feel they have some right to be violent. Typically, this is due to the people around them. An atmosphere of hatred or perversion sometimes riles the demons up as they are cast out. In this case, they will try to cause pain to the person they have been tormenting or the deliverance minister.

Just as a sheriff carries a sidearm when handling evictions, the deliverance minister should be armed with the Sword of the Spirit and the shield of faith to withstand the enemy's attacks.

DELIVERANCE NEEDS INNER HEALING

Deliverance is the removal of infection from a wound. Removing the infection is only one step in the process of treatment. If deliverance is done without healing, then the enemy will come back. The wounds of rejection, shame, and insecurity must be treated and allowed to heal. This, in turn, will prevent the enemy from having a place to return to. (See Chapter 7 on inner healing.)

Several years ago, on the way home from a ladies' retreat, God activated The Father's House in the ministry of deliverance. They were in the middle of an eight-hour drive, worshipping the Lord and praying together. I've been told the atmosphere was electric. Suddenly, one of the ladies began to feel extreme discomfort. Things escalated as she shared with the ladies the symptoms she was experiencing. The ladies began to pray for her, and demons began to manifest. Voices that were not hers came out of her while her face contorted in dozens of different expressions. Armed with little experience or training but filled with faith, the ladies persisted, praying and making declarations over their sister. This lady belonged to Jesus, and Satan could not have her! After several hours, the van shook, and a swirl of light encircled the outside of the entire van. The lady was released, and the demon left. Exhausted but overjoyed, the whole van returned to their worship, galvanized as a team that would protect each other against whatever Satan threw their way.

That lady has been a member of The Father's House since it began and has been a Christian for over 30 years. Yet the enemy had found a place in her life from where he could control areas of her emotions and make continual accusations against her mind. But a van full of Spirit-filled ladies knocked him out in less than three hours.

Stories like this often cause believers to ask, "Do I have a demon?" The answer is found by looking at our wounds.

DO YOU HAVE UNTREATED WOUNDS?

In searching for the infections of the soul that demons bring, we've learned to look for wounds. While there are many ways that our souls can be wounded in this fallen world, there are seven common ones that we walk our people through in times of prayer and ministry. They are bitterness, witchcraft, sexual sin, religion, generational sin, trauma, and inner vows.

BITTERNESS

When we fail to forgive an offense, the offense grows infected with bitterness. The most common place of demonic activity in a believer's life is in the area of forgiveness. The Cross is what makes this so. When you receive the gift of Christ's forgiveness through His atoning work on Calvary, you agree never again to withhold forgiveness. Any refusal to forgive is an act of treason in the Kingdom of Heaven and sentences us to great pain at the hands of tormentors, aka demons. Jesus spells out this principle in one of His parables.[41] A man forgiven of a massive debt imprisons a man who owes him a minuscule debt. Upon finding this out, the King throws this thankless man into the same prison. Bitterness against another believer is an expression of ingratitude towards Christ's work on the Cross.

Do you hold resentment in your heart towards someone? It's time to forgive. Here's another way to ask it. Fill in the blank. The person I need to forgive the most is _____. Who came to mind?

It's time to forgive them. This is a big deal. See Chapter 8 for more.

---

41 Matthew 18:21-35.

SEXUAL SIN

The Apostle Paul sets sexual sin apart from other sins by calling it a sin against our own bodies. Sex is a physical action that has a spiritual result, and sexual sin creates an exchange not only in the physical world but also in the spiritual realm. Many people go through life unaware of all the spiritual attachments they have with former sexual partners. Their fornication has opened doors in their lives where they carry the demonic torment that their partner had along with their own. Pornography isn't any better. It's fornication through a different avenue. The eyes are the windows to the soul, and continual participation in porn invites evil spirits to take up habitation in the thought life of the culprit.

Sadly, much of the church is ill-equipped to deal with sexual sin. There've been too many scandals and not enough conversation. It's become the last place a Christian wants to open up and seek help.

The solutions that so many offer deal only with the symptoms. Sexual sin invites the enemy to operate in the flesh. The enemy must be removed for this habitual sin of the flesh to be overcome.

Jesus is so tender towards the humble. When a person humbly speaks out the ways they've sinned in this area and repents before the Lord, peace washes over them profoundly. It is a simple matter, then, for a prayer team member to command the different spirits of perversion that have been present to leave and go to the Cross. More often than not, sexual sin is a "fruit" problem and not a "root" problem. I often have people who come for prayer and deliverance who think that their biggest problem is the bondage they have in the area of sexual perversion. They are stunned when the Holy Spirit reveals the actual roots of why they struggle with intimacy, lust, and shame. When the demons are silenced, the confusion is lifted, and they can begin the journey of allowing the Lord to lead them into healthy sexuality.

WITCHCRAFT

Witchcraft is on the rise in America. What was once a mostly unacknowledged small presence in the religious world of this country has become mainstream. Our ministry has cast devils out that got involved through horror movies, Ouija boards, séances, fortune-telling, ghost hunting, shamanism, Free-Masonry, and much more. One church called us because they were struggling to help a family that had visited one of their services. The parents shared that they had found their six-month-old baby levitating in the air multiple times, and thinking that it was cool, had been posting videos of it to social media. Things had turned dark quickly, and now the baby was clearly being emotionally tormented, unable to sleep or be calmed. I asked if any items in the house had been dedicated to evil spirits. They responded that a week before these events had begun, a relative had given them a shaman's staff that he claimed contained powers associated with Native American spirits. We prayed. They got rid of the staff. The baby went back to being calm. Both parents got saved and began following Jesus! Hallelujah!

Actions that expose us to the spirit world and items dedicated to evil spirits can open us up to terrible torment.

Repent for the action. Remove and destroy any related items. Invite Jesus into the situation while commanding any spirits that oppose Him to leave and go to the Cross.

RELIGION

Frankly, witchcraft and false religion are both forms of idolatry, but whenever we ask people if they have a history of idolatry, they would tell us no. False religion invites demonic involvement. Jesus spoke of the Leaven of the Pharisees and warned of the hypocrisy that they operated in. He called these same Pharisees sons of the Devil! That sounds like demons might be present. Jesus warned of false prophets and deceivers appearing as angels of light. Paul wrote of forms of godliness that denied God's power, and John wrote extensively to combat heresies about Christ's identity. There is a lot of bad religion, even in Christianity. Conservative Christianity often has forms of legalism and performance. Liberal Christianity offers a license to sin. At the same time, some charismatic-minded Christians have opened doors to New Age practices. I've cast demons out of believers from about every denomination you could name. It's surprisingly easy to go to church but not keep your faith in Jesus, which leads to idolatry and demonic oppression. You can be born again but remain in bondage.

GENERATIONAL SIN

Generational Sin is a concept only discussed in the Old Testament,[42] and therefore ignored by much of the Body of Christ. However, it is a principle that is seen in other parts of life. Cessationists[43] don't argue with their doctor when asked to give a family history. They know that heart disease or certain types of cancer can be genetic. Because the Bible plainly teaches the concept, though only in the Old Testament, and because of the logic of it, not to mention the experiences I've had with it, it is safe to say it's a significant area of demonic activity in people's lives. Consider the story of my former student, our real-life example from the beginning of this chapter. The addiction of his father and the impartation of his mother caused a demon that he had not invited through any actions of his own. I've seen people healed of cancer after individuals renounced the agreements that previous generations of family had made with secret societies like Free-Masonry. The concept of generational sin is also supported by the laws of nature. The law of sowing and reaping tells us that if sin is sown into a family, it will reap a terrible harvest. The law of "producing after kinds" shows us that what is joined together is reproduced. When two people covenant to cover up sin, the offspring of this covenant will reflect that sin and will be uncontrollable and uncontainable.

---

42 Exodus 20:5-6.

43 In Christianity, a cessationist is someone who believes the supernatural gifts, signs and wonders, and (in some cases) demonic manifestations have all ceased with the death of the 12 apostles and the formation of Scripture.

TRAUMA

Trauma is the wounding of the soul, and as any soul wound, can be infected by the enemy. My wife, Candace, has had two traumatic car accidents 22 years apart. Each accident left wounds in her heart that caused fear. This fear would manifest in stressful seasons and incapacitate her from doing even basic things. When the trauma from these accidents was dealt with, the panic attacks went away. In my own life, I discovered a fear of failure that came from the traumatic experiences of seeing my father fired, investigated, incarcerated, and sentenced. The conversations, FBI raid, media coverage, and hearings in a federal courthouse were all more traumatic than I initially realized. Only recently have I been able to experience healing and release from the emotional turmoil of that season. Military veterans with PTSD, abuse survivors, and those grieving untimely deaths of loved ones are common examples of people who have been severely traumatized. Deliverance is only one piece of what is needed, and in many cases it is not the first piece. Therapy, counseling, and a healthy community are all necessary components for their complete recovery.

There are people who don't believe that complete recovery is possible from some traumatic events. While I sympathize with the severity of pain that many have experienced, I believe in the total healing power of Jesus, regardless of the situation. It may take time. It may require a team. But Jesus will use His people and His compassion to bring about total healing.

INNER VOWS

An inner vow is simply a hidden internal law that we have chosen to live by. If one of your parents told you that you reminded them of your other parent while painting them in a negative light, you may have made an inner vow never to be like that particular parent. The problem with that is wherever our attention is, our direction becomes. In order to avoid becoming like that parent, we constantly look at their negative traits and resent them. Each look and each advancement of resentment only drives the image of their negativity deeper into our souls, eventually forming us into the very thing we despise. When we obtain our driver's licenses, we learn quickly that we have to keep our eyes on where we want to end up, not on what we want to avoid. The driver who looks at the ditch on the left in order to avoid it, often ends up in the ditch on the right. Ironically, attempting to avoid a ditch put them in a ditch. Inner vows are labels we put on ourselves, comparisons that we make, and oaths that we swear. In each case, they are false gods. Our eyes must be put on Jesus. He is our model and example. His walk with Abba is the journey we must emulate. Anything else is a ditch that will swallow us up.

While there are many other areas in our lives where the enemy may attack, these seven cover the vast majority of places where we see demonization.

Freedom is not the final step in the journey of following Jesus. The Jews, whom God delivered from Egypt with Moses as their leader, were freed from bondage but needed to change the way they thought. They continued in the wilderness with a "slave mentality" of fear and unhealthy dependence. Some ministries only do deliverance. Discipleship, the work of training and sanctification in a local church, is a major component in helping freed people stay free. *"For freedom, Christ set us free. Stand firm, then, and don't submit again to a yoke of slavery."* (Galatians 5:1, CSB)

PRAYER OF DELIVERANCE

Father,

In the mighty name of Jesus, I claim all the freedom that was purchased for me on the Cross. Holy Spirit, I ask you to expose any stronghold or lie that the enemy has placed in my life. I plead the blood against every scheme, weapon, or demon that is coming against me, and I ask you, Father, to lead me to complete victory through the truth of your Word, the power of the resurrection, and the authority of your name.

Amen

CHAPTER 6

THE SPIRIT OF ADOPTION

> *"I got into a cold state. It did not seem as if there was any unction resting upon my ministry. For four long months God seemed to be just showing me myself. I found I was ambitious; I was not preaching for Christ; I was preaching for ambition. I found everything in my heart that ought not to be there. For four months, a wrestling went on within me, and I was a miserable man. But after four months, the anointing came."*
> —DL Moody

If ever a man needed a special touch of the Master's hand, Moody did. That gift came one day while he walked the streets of New York to the house of a friend. "God Almighty seemed to come very near," Moody recalled. "I felt I must be alone." He hurried to the house of his friend nearby, was shown upstairs, and, on entering, quickly asked, half-apologizing: "I need to be alone. Have you a room I can use?" Moody's host graciously showed him to a room without delay. He entered, closed the door, and sat on a sofa—and then went to his knees. Almost instantly, he had a deep, unmistakable sense of the presence of God. Words nearly failed Moody when he tried to tell what happened next. "Ah, what a day!" he remembered. "I cannot describe it. I seldom refer to it, it is almost too sacred an experience to name—Paul had an experience of which he never spoke for fourteen years—I can only say God revealed Himself to me, and I had such an experience of His love that I had to ask Him to stay His hand. [After this,] I went to preaching again. The sermons were not different. I did not present any new truths. Yet hundreds were converted. I would not now be placed back where I was, before that blessed experience, if you should give me all the world." As one writer memorably phrased it: Moody had been given a personal Pentecost, an experience literally in an upper room. "Many a time I have thought of it since," Moody said some years later. "I was wretched no longer ... If I have not been a different man since, I do not know myself ... There was a time when I wanted [only] to see my little vineyard blessed, and I could not get out of it. But I could work for the whole world now ... go round the world, and tell the perishing millions of a Savior's love." When Moody needed Him most, God came. In mercy, he was given a lasting sense of grace and peace. He felt renewed and strengthened as he never had before. One sentence captured what he felt: "I was all the time tugging and carrying water. But now I have a river that carries me." For the rest of his life, this profound sense of God's presence and power shaped Moody's ministry.[44]

Very few men have impacted the English-speaking world of Protestant Christianity like D.L. Moody. By the time he had his "Pentecostal" experience, he had already preached across America and throughout Great Britain. He had planted churches, started schools, and held evangelistic campaigns that reached thousands for Christ.

Yet something was missing in Mr. Moody's life. He had been profoundly shaped by the Gospel, given a sense of urgency and mission and

44 Belmonte, Kevin. *D.L. Moody—A Life: Innovator, Evangelist, World Changer* (pp. 105-106). Moody Publishers, Kindle Edition.

a profound passion for rescuing sinners from Hell. His ministry was producing incredible fruit. He was well-respected, successful, and blessed by the Lord. Still, he needed something more. He needed a fresh touch of the Father's Love.

I was sitting on a plane with my oldest son, Kenny, reading Moody's biography when I came across this story. I had previously read several other biographical excerpts of Moody's life, but it struck me differently this time. A man who preached the Gospel with exceptional effectiveness needed a *baptism* of love. A man who was already filled with the unction of the Holy Spirit needed still another experience.

I thought of the trip that I had just enjoyed with Kenny. For his 12th birthday, I took him to Colorado to hike and to talk. As we enjoyed our days together, I had shared my heart with him. I was transparent about the challenges of manhood and the struggles of many in my family. But I affirmed him. I introduced him to God-fearing manhood. I presented the joy of being a loving husband and a committed father. I shared some of the victories I had experienced in my walk with Jesus, and I challenged him to surpass me. I assured him that he had a Dad in me, a Friend in Jesus, and a Father in God that would help him become an even more incredible person than he already was. That week, Kenny experienced my love in a new way. With words on hikes and over steak dinners, he was given a clear path forward for life and a confidence that he was seen and would be cared for as he continued on this adventure of being a Christ-honoring man. Kenny already knew I loved him, but this experience was different. I hope it was a powerful relational experience that shaped him in a way that will forever point him to Abba.

As I was on this journey of discovering more of the Holy Spirit, experiencing the love of God afresh had not been on my list of pursuits. Looking back, it is painfully evident that I needed it. Through the disappointments I had experienced, I had allowed discouragement to encroach and was operating as a spiritual orphan. This attitude made me defensive, overly sensitive, and fearful. I made each decision, anticipating that it would be rejected.

Our world is filled with rejection. It is a spirit that drives nearly everything we do. Since Adam and Eve were cast out of the Garden, since Cain's offering was not accepted, and since Abel suffered the violent consequences of a jealous older brother, rejection has continually grown as a force of evil on this planet. Religion hasn't helped either. Anthropologists and historians seem to agree that most of the wars and conflicts that rage on the earth have religion as a primary root. Many of us live under the spirit of Cain. We feel that our offering isn't good enough. We strive to please God but often self-sabotage our efforts, knowing in our subconscious that what we have to offer Him is terribly lacking. Religion, including many forms of Christianity, is filled with performance. Though most Christians believe in a salvation of grace, they practice a sonship of works. We are the older brothers in the parable of the Prodigal Son. We work faithfully but don't seem to be noticed or celebrated by God. God seems pretty distant—an afar off God, busy with others, choosing broken people to fashion into trophies of grace while ignoring the brokenness that we feel inside our hearts. Deep down, we feel rejected by God. We believe that He doesn't care much for our offerings. And if we're honest, he doesn't care much about us. It's a lie that we don't believe theologically, but despite learning "Jesus Loves Me" as children, it remains planted in the soil of our inner man—a damning core belief that the God who died for us in the past wants nothing to do with us in the present.

Over the past four years, I've spoken to well over 100 pastors personally about this topic. As they've gotten candid with me, the overwhelming majority of them have admitted that based on their experiences and emotions, they don't feel that God loves them very much. Men ordained to be loving shepherds and representatives of an all-powerful and all-loving God are leading the sheep under a spirit of rejection.

The God of love has been distorted in our churches. Either He's a God of license that allows us to continue in sin, or He's a God of law that looks at us with fiery anger at every stumble we make. Those who abuse His grace fall under the rejection that comes with the shameful consequences of their actions. Perversion, addiction, and greed each invite voices of shame to taunt us and hinder us from hearing God's tender voice.

On the other hand, those who live under God's Law busy themselves to the point of exhaustion, burning out to meet God's demands. Eventually, they feel used and abused, tired of serving a task-master who never seems pleased.

The Bride of Jesus needs a baptism of holy love—this is what Mr. Moody experienced in a borrowed upper room in New York City. After losing his home and all of the ministry buildings that he had built to the Chicago Fire, he felt apathetic towards the prospect of raising funds again and rebuilding. His heart was cold and his soul weary. Then God's love fell on him.

All around the world, the church is faced with rebuilding. The fires of conflict, pandemic, polarization, and spiritual wickedness have burned our works down and left us hurting. The pain has gone untreated for so long that we have become fearful of what it will take for us to rebuild. The spirit of rejection has set in like a pervasive darkness in the hearts of many believers. The fragility of our faith has been exposed. The idea of forging ahead in bold faith seems too painful and costly.

The spirit of rejection is effective in only showing us the cost of commitment. It warns our wounded hearts not to trust God because He will only disappoint you, or worse, you'll be found quite disappointing to Him. It tells us not to try, for failure will be our certain result. Rejection takes the romance out of life by showing us all the nasty distortions of love. Rape, perversion, abuse, infidelity, and apathy all serve as examples of where love will get you. Rejection preaches a message of hopelessness, and those who listen to it live in despair.

We see the fruit of rejection played out in the life of Jacob, the Old Testament patriarch. Jacob was rejected by his father, Isaac, who preferred the more masculine elder son, Esau. Everything Jacob did seemed to be an attempt to grab honor and love from his father. He bargained for and obtained the birthright of the eldest from Esau. With his mother's help, he disguised himself as Esau and stole his brother's blessing, deceiving a blinded Isaac.

But it caught up to him. He moved away to work for his uncle and fell in love with the youngest daughter, Rachel. Desperate to marry her, Jacob agreed to work seven years for Laban to earn Rachel's hand in marriage. The time flew by as he worked under the law of love. But when the morning after the marriage came, Jacob woke up to see the face of Leah. The wedding traditions were such that the face of the bride had been covered. Jacob's eyes had been taken off of Rachel, and now he had awoken to a truth that left him feeling cheated and angry.

I believe Jacob is a picture of many Christians today. They have worked under the impression that they would earn the affections of the Lord, only to experience a wake-up call of disappointment. The name "Rachel" means "ewe lamb," and the name Leah means "weariness." It's a powerful metaphor for the way that the church is feeling in this season. The traditions of man have caused many to take their eyes off the Lamb, and they have awakened to weariness. They have lost their first love, and the fatigue and rejection they feel has them believing that they cannot go on. The Church of Jesus needs a baptism of holy love.

In September 2020, I flew to Atlanta to prevent a friend from joining a cult. Josh Smith is the pastor of Cowan Mill Church in Douglasville, Georgia, and one of my best friends in the world. In 2017, I had shared with him my experience of finding freedom in the Holy Spirit and receiving the gift of speaking in tongues. His response was a mixture of disbelief, intrigue, and bewilderment.

Josh is Southern to the core, a larger-than-life character with a massive heart of compassion for people that has impacted thousands of lives across the United States and West Africa. Yet, in that season, his own ministry had hit a dry spell. Now, his Baptist friend was telling him he'd been baptized in the Spirit, and signs and wonders were beginning to happen. Determined to see if it was true for himself, Josh went on a pursuit of the Holy Spirit that would transform his church and his entire town.

Three years into the journey, Josh had called Jerod and me and invited us to try out a retreat called "Holy Spirit Encounter" in North Georgia. Josh is quick to try anything, and I felt like he might be on the wrong track with this idea. The name Holy Spirit Encounter sounded like a cheap thrill ride at a Christian theme park that came with 3D glasses. Boy, was I wrong.

As I went through the different aspects of the retreat, I found it somewhat basic. Session after session taught on the ministry of the Holy Spirit—things that I had already been discovering and experiencing over the years. After a few sessions, the group of 30 men went into a chapel for worship and prayer. While worship videos played on large television screens, God began to speak to me. "I love you," He said. Over and over again, in the two hours of worship and prayer, He kept repeating Himself. "I love you. I love you. I love you."

Though I was several years into fellowship with the Holy Spirit, it was apparent that the Lord wanted me to fall into His love. During the second day of the retreat, the "love awakening" continued. The basic teaching continued, but the lessons hit me differently, with the soundtrack of God's voice on repeat in my head. "I love you, Ken, " He said over and over again.

In chapel that evening, God broke something off me. Pastor Jewell, the director of the ministry, stepped up to me, placed his hands on me, and began praying. A wave of God's love washed over me. To this day, I couldn't tell you what he prayed, but I'll always remember how God's voice sounded and how His love felt. I collapsed to the floor and lay there a long time as God did spiritual surgery on me. He took the self-reliance, the defensiveness, the fear, and the shame away and washed over me with His love.

The morning after I got home from the retreat, my heart was still beating to the rhythm of God's love message. I felt euphoric. I began to testify to Candace about what had happened, and then the message of God's love in my heart shifted. Now it said, "Love her."

"Love her?" What does that mean?

"Tell her you're sorry," the Spirit replied.

Suddenly, my spiritual eyes were opened, and I could see all the pain my struggles and disappointments had caused Candace. I could see how my anger and lust had wounded her over the years. I felt like my heart was touching hers and feeling all the anguish that being married to me had brought. I began to weep and apologize, and when I ran out of words, I just lay at her feet praying.

We prayed together in our room that day for over ten hours. Now that I trusted God's love for me, He could gently lead me to begin dealing with the effects my brokenness had on others. God healed my marriage that day. Years before, while painting a bathroom, He'd fallen on us and led us each into a deeper understanding of Him, but now He was washing us in His love and healing our feelings toward each other.

When we live under a spirit of rejection, we cannot have healthy relationships or hear God's gentle voice. Every syllable we hear uttered under rejection triggers fear. The constant state of fear makes us run, and we live in spiritual states of survival and self-preservation. We are orphans, looking out for ourselves, believing that no one cares for us, and dreading the imminent pain and ruin that we know is lurking behind every corner. Then perfect love comes.

The cure for rejection is adoption. Romans 8:15 (NLT).

So you have not received a spirit that makes you fearful slaves. Instead, you received God's Spirit when he adopted you as his own children. Now we call him, "Abba, Father."

When an orphan is adopted into a healthy situation, he encounters a person who chooses him and commits to responsibility for his health and well-being. It seems too good to be true. The idea of being transferred from the streets of self-preservation to the safety of home and the unconditional love of family is transformational.

In my experience, the love of God came to me and began to shift my mindset. Like the parable of the prodigal son, I had allowed the dreadful state of my spiritual life to cause me to believe that I could only be a slave for God, performing all of His wishes in hopes of earning His favor. But God, who is rich in mercy, refused my handshake deal and threw His arms around me. He celebrated me! I can still see the vision in my spirit as I write this: Me standing there in a tattered garment, filthy from the life choices I had made. Him dancing around me with loud exclamations of joy and affirmation, giving me a new robe to wear.

Ken came home! Oh, what a wonderful day! My son was lost, but now he is found! He was dead, but here he stands before me, alive! Let's celebrate! Get the best of everything for the one who has my heart has returned and will be with me forever!"

If you've been a Christian for any length of time, you may find some objections rising up in you at the idea of some of the things I've written. God dancing around us sounds pretty narcissistic. After all, the Bible is the revelation of Jesus, not the revelation of us. Many in today's American church have cheapened grace in such a way that it does seem like God is here for us, like some lovesick, lonely God desperate for any attention that we might throw His way.

That's where the Father must come in. The baptism of love can only come in when we see God our Father as the One who truly loves and calls us to Himself. He is not desperate. He is, however, wild.

I love being a Dad. I have four wonderful kids, and their ages this year, in particular, are quite challenging. Kenny is fourteen this year. He is a serious-minded freshman in high school who reminds me in his own mindset of my tendency to take life and myself too seriously. He stresses about upcoming tests, though he tends to ace them. He worries about the cost of things, though we live a very comfortable life. He even laments time wasted over trivial things when more important things could have been tended to. He gets all of this from me. Looking at him, I see a reflection of my own struggles with life's tasks. As his dad, I work to free him from those traps. That's where my youngest comes in.

Claire is six, and as serious as Kenny can be, is as light-hearted and giggly as she can be. For Claire, Kenny is the perfect older brother. They share the same genetic illness, and Kenny is often helping her understand the process for self-care treatments that will be most effective. For Kenny, Claire is the smile that he needs. Her giggles and silly jokes break his serious thoughts. Her little dances on our living room floor cause him to forget his own adolescent insecurities and to swing around, his long arms sweeping around as his body twirls next to her. Her childishness makes him act wild. Unrestrained, uninhibited, and filled with joy, together they laugh in playful, silly dance moves that make my heart beat with delight. These are my children, and I am so pleased with them. My other two kids soon jump in. My daughter Chloe, a worship warrior for Jesus, singing and sashaying across the floor, and my son Clarke grabbing a spatula and pot from the kitchen to hammer out an extra drum beat that only he thought was missing from the music. As I watch them, I join them, and I laugh and dance and love *wildly*.

THE WILD LOVE OF GOD

The picture of the Father in the Scriptures seems to be this incredibly serious and purposed God who, on many occasions, sees His children and joins them to love them wildly. In Genesis, He came to Abraham and enjoyed steak and gravy-covered biscuits before sharing his heart with him concerning the events of Sodom.[45] He looks like a Father who stays up late after a meal, sharing a little more than he should with a son in whom He delights.

In Joshua 10, He steps in almost a little too defensively in a lengthy battle. Watching his children duke it out with some giants, He steps in and starts throwing God-sized hail stones, taking out more enemy soldiers than all of the Jewish warriors combined. At Solomon's dedication of the Temple,[46] he almost gets a little too excited, filling the temple with such Glory that the 120 priests fall down in awe and probably a little fear. The presence of the Infinite touching a dwelling place made with human hands and shaking it with the eminence of His aura. The prophet Zephaniah portrays him as a Father who cradles his child and sings the wild songs of a doting Dad over the cooing cries of a restless toddler.[47]

When Jesus comes, the *wildness* continues. His forerunner is a wilderness eccentric. His approach to wedding parties is to lengthen their duration by doubling their wine supply. His companions in ministry have colorful and even scandalous pasts. He walks on water because He can. He tells storms to knock it off. He defies the religious systems. He heals his captor's severed ear. Even after death, he stops a parade to Heaven to comfort a grief-stricken and bewildered Mary—the one whom He delivered from seven devils.

---

45 See Genesis 18.

46 I Kings 8 & 2 Chronicles 7.

47 Zephaniah 3:17.

In His final words to His disciples, He tells them that He is the image of the Father. The way He walks and talks and everything He has done is because that is the way His Father would do it! That means that if Abba had been at that wedding party in Cana where the wine ran out, He would've done the same thing Jesus did!

The love of the Father is more incredible than you've ever imagined, and He has adopted you!

THE SPIRIT OF THE WILD ONE IS IN YOU

Along with the Cross, the greatest revelation of God's love is the Gift of the Holy Spirit.

Consider Luke's words,

What father among you, if his son asks for a fish, will instead of a fish give him a serpent; or if he asks for an egg, will give him a scorpion? If you then, who are evil, know how to give good gifts to your children, how much more will the heavenly Father give the Holy Spirit to those who ask him! (Luke 11:11–13, ESV)

The Apostle Paul speaks about this in Romans 5:5:

And this hope will not lead to disappointment. For we know how dearly God loves us, because he has given us the Holy Spirit to fill our hearts with his love.

One reason the spirit of rejection is so prevalent in the Body of Christ is that they have lost the joy found in the Gift of the Holy Spirit. If we lose sight of the gift, a time will come when we forget the love behind it. We must remain focused on the Presence of the Spirit. He is the manifestation of Abba Father's love for us and the Spirit of Jesus within us! The exact powerful yet joyful nature that Jesus possessed is now poured into us as an active living Person, tied to our spirits and continuously reminding us of Abba's love.

As I've continued this journey, I've found that the enemy continually offers me "off ramps" from the river of Abba's love. It is easy to neglect spiritual rest, to fall for the trap of being needed, and to return to a spirit of performance, striving to please everyone while ignoring the internal whisper of God. Jesus, in His infinite wisdom, knew this would be the case for anyone who tried to follow Him, so He gave us a few simple steps to follow that would keep us in His perfect love. They are Abide, Receive, Listen, Love, and Obey.

Abide: *As the Father has loved me, so have I loved you. Abide in my love.* (John 15:9)

The ability to stay grounded in God's love begins with purposed thoughts. Meditating on the truths of God's Word and reflecting on His goodness begin a regular process that draws my wandering spirit back into the familiar doorframe of the family of God. It is so easy to get caught up with thoughts of work, worry, and responsibility that I wander away from the comforting awareness of God's Presence and get caught up in the enemy's distracting imaginations. Abiding is stilling ourselves in the truth of God until we are brought into a renewed awareness of His Presence. When we are with Him and aware of it, we are safe. The truth that God will never leave us is unconditional, but we tend to become unaware of him and drift into deception. The danger of our Western way of "doing church" is that it disconnects us from so many avenues of abiding. When we disconnect from the community in the Body, we lose fellowship, communion, exhortation, and correction and severely limit the ways that we can abide.

Abiding calls us not only to gathering but also to imagining Him. The Scriptures are filled with imagery that can serve as breadcrumbs for our imagination. Have you ever taken the time to imagine what the door of your heart might look like and what it sounds like in your spirit to have Jesus knocking on it? Have you considered what it would take to open that door and what His face would look like on the other side? As I abide in Him, I've seen Him as the slain Lamb. Blood covers His face, a graphic image of the cost of my sin, and I feel an indescribable awe that wrecks me as He takes His hand, rubs it on His forehead, and wipes His blood across my face. "Worthy is the Lamb that was slain!"

Other times of dwelling in His presence have presented Him as the King of Glory. I come into agreement with John's image and see Jesus with eyes that emanate fire. The words from His mouth pierce my heart, and I fall before Him. Kneeling in worshipful adoration, I see words written on His thigh. I turn them into a prayer. "You are my King of kings, and you are my Lord of lords."[48] For more on this, see Chapter 10.

Receive: *...Ask, and you will receive, that your joy may be full.* (John 16:24)

If you want to experience the love of the Father, you must be willing to receive. A massive joy of childhood is found in allowing your parents to love you through giving. God is a Giver. He loves to give! Some theologians portray us as selfish because we dare ask for more than we've already been given. But the Scriptures paint a different picture. If He spared not His own Son, won't He freely give us all things?[49] The Father, who paid an infinite price to adopt us, continues to display an eternally generous heart by pouring gifts of favor on us. As we abide in His love, we will learn to ask. As our love matures, the kind of things we ask for may change. However, we must never stop asking. Asking is an act of faith and trust that says, "Abba, I know you love me and will freely give me all things, so here I come with childlike faith."

A danger of maturity is losing the ability to receive lavish love. If you came to me and offered me the keys and title to your car, my adult sensibilities would cause me to hesitate and most likely reject it. If you offered the same to my 10-year-old son, Clarke, he'd take it. He enjoys lavish love and is shameless in receiving. Continually receiving from the Father keeps us in a joyful state of child-like faith.

---

48 See Revelation 19:11-16.
49 See Romans 8:32.

Listen: *The Holy Spirit will teach you all things and bring to your remembrance all that I have said to you.* (John 14:26)

Family isn't only about receiving. There's a lot of talking that happens! As I write this, I anticipate my children coming home from school and interrupting me. I welcome this interruption because I love their presence. Their interruption will come with words. They will want to tell me about their day and ask me about mine.

One of the dreaded events in our home is bedtime. My kids have learned that one way to stay up later is to ask me questions about the Bible or other spiritual matters. Listening to me allows them more access to me. As Jesus prepared for His death, He spoke to His disciples about his relationship with Him and His Father through the Holy Spirit. These men had spent the last three years learning from Him, and now, at the hour of His departure, He promised them that the relationship would continue. Through the Spirit, they would learn, experience the presence of the Father, and know what to do. Whenever I feel distant from the Lord, I turn to Him in a time of abiding and ask Him questions. My desire to hear Him opens up access to Him, and I find comfort in His words.

Love: *He who loves me will be loved by my Father, and I will love him and manifest myself to him.* (John 14:21)

Love one another as I have loved you. (John 15:12)

Often, in my times of abiding, the Lord will bring someone to mind who needs encouragement. This is the tender nature of God. He loves others through us. His voice of direction makes us feel loved. Our delivery of the message makes the recipient feel loved.

It is so easy to switch into a spirit of obligation that worries about what other people think and allow that to be our motivation for reaching out to people. We need to be *in* the love of Abba in order to have His heart of love for people.

Obey: *If anyone loves me, he will keep my word, and my Father will love him, and we will come to him and make our home with him.* (John 14:23)

Living under the spirit of adoption requires obedience. As we listen, a seed is planted. As we obey, fruit begins to appear. One of my favorite Biblical examples of obedience is found in the story of a young girl named Mary. As Gabriel appears and gives her an overwhelming and eternity-shaking word, she simply replies, "Tell me how," and, "Let it be." Childlike obedience is found here. When the Lord tells you to do something, ask Him how to do it and commit to doing it.

"Tell me how."

"Let it be."

Though I have come quite a long way in this journey of being loved by Abba, I am still quite far from perfect. It is so easy in difficult seasons to allow stress and conflict to draw me into choppy seas of uncertainty and fear. Waves of doubt and insecurity wash over me, and the enemy howls accusations and threats that tempt me to despair. In all the noise, a small, inner voice speaks, reminding me of the One with whom I abide. When I call His name, He silences the storm. He gives me rest. He washes me in His love. The love of Abba brings peace.

Abba,

In the name of Jesus, I kneel before you. Help me know the love of Christ that surpasses understanding. May my heart be stretched in every direction with the fullness of your love. Expose any lie in me that suppresses your love, and baptize me in the deepest parts of your affection. As I heal in your love, allow me to reflect it and demonstrate it to others.

Amen

CHAPTER 7

WHEN GOD ALWAYS HEALS

THE POWER OF INNER HEALING

> *Captivity is a type of bondage from which a person cannot break free by willpower alone. In our present world, it manifests itself in a wide spectrum of problems: people pleasing; driven-ness; eating disorders; sexual compulsivity; and persistent emotional patterns of anxiety, fear, anger, or depression. I have an addictive personality and have been captive to many bondages: cigarettes, drugs, excessive drinking, sexual impurity, workaholism, drivenness, and enslaving beliefs such as feeling as though I don't belong.*[50]
>
> Rusty Rustenbach

---

[50] Rustenbach, Rusty. A Guide for Listening and Inner-Healing Prayer: Meeting God in the Broken Places (p. 30). The Navigators, Kindle Edition.

Psalm 147:3–5 (ESV): *He heals the brokenhearted and binds up their wounds. He determines the number of the stars; he gives to all of them their names. Great is our Lord, and abundant in power; his understanding is beyond measure.*

In 2020, I got extremely sick. I was weakened to the point of limited mobility. For nearly two months, everything I ate made me sick, and most days I couldn't keep food down. I was in extreme pain and lost an unhealthy amount of weight. As the weeks went on, I began to wonder if I'd ever be able to eat normally again. It was extremely discouraging. During a season when millions around the world were dealing with Covid-19, I was dealing with what doctors said were severe gallbladder attacks. The only recommendation from doctors was to remove the gallbladder. Scans showed that it was full of gallstones and there was nothing else they could do. I began a season of fasting followed by an extremely bland diet, and though all the joy of eating was taken away from me, the pain was finally manageable. Most meals were still accompanied with ibuprofen, and other medications were always nearby.

It was during this time that I found myself standing in a prayer line before a volunteer pastor. It was the first night of Holy Spirit Encounter (see previous chapter), and I felt out of place and unsure of what I'd gotten myself into. After a time of worship, we had been invited to seek out one of the volunteer leaders at the front of the room and ask for prayer for anything we might need. I needed healing from gallbladder disease. Though I'd already prayed for my share of sick people, I still felt foolish as I went to the front and asked a total stranger to pray for my healing. He looked me in the eyes as I spoke and put his hand on my chest. "Ken, your problem isn't in your gallbladder, it's right here." He said while looking at his hand resting over my heart. "When you get your heart healed from bitterness, you're gallbladder will be just fine."

I stepped back, somewhat offended. This man did not know me. We had never met. How dare he make assumptions about my heart! Working through the emotions and the initial pride, I allowed him to finish praying for me and left the service. The next day I sat with three more volunteer ministers in a session that they referred to as a "prayer room." They asked me questions about my past. "Have you experienced anything traumatic in your life? Is there anyone who has hurt you that continually comes to your mind? Is there sexual sin or other bondage that you want to be free of?"

As I gave answers, they would say simple prayers over me, remind of a Biblical truth or passage, and move on to the next question. As the meeting went on, the questions became more specific. It was as if someone was feeding them information about my life, but the information they were getting wasn't known by anyone other than my wife. By the time the session was over, I was weeping. Three gentle people had allowed me to confess my faults to them and had ministered in response with the forgiveness of Jesus and the love of Abba. In less than ninety minutes, decades of emotional turmoil, regret, and shame were canceled out through the power of the Holy Spirit. I walked out of the room lighter than I could ever remember feeling. My inner man had experienced healing.

WHAT IS INNER HEALING?

Inner healing or, "healing for the inner man," is simply the process of inviting Jesus to heal the wounds of a person's heart and soul so that the Spirit may lead them.

Inner healing ministry involves helping people identify the curses and consequences that have come upon them due to their actions and those of family and friends and helping them find freedom and healing from those curses. Sometimes, the client finds Jesus for the first time and is born again. In other cases, the client is helped to see that the inheritance they received through salvation has been severely limited by the laws of sin and death that remain partially in place over their lives. Inner healing ministry is simply helping people encounter the Truth. This Truth encounter is really a Jesus encounter. Just as in the Gospels, whenever the sick encountered Jesus in faith, they were healed.

THE NECESSITY OF INNER HEALING IN THE SOUL OF MAN

Just as our physical bodies have many parts and systems, our inner man has many parts and systems. To keep things simple, we often refer to the inner man as the soul.[51] The soul of man contains his mind, will, emotions, memories, and imagination. That is our thoughts, decisions, feelings, past, core beliefs, and goals. The heart is the "engine" that takes all of these parts and creates actions and processes. Think of the soul as a building with many rooms. Each room has computers, machines, and tools that fabricate and repair things. Think of the heart as the electrical supply to the building. Without power, the rooms are dark, and the various machines and tools are useless, but if the power is turned on, everything can operate as it should.

Ideally, the soul of man should look like this:

- His mind is filled with truth.

- His will is filled with wisdom.

- His emotions are filled with love and understanding.

- His memories are filled with remembrances of Father God's goodness and faithfulness.

- His imaginations are filled with confidence in his place in the family of God, self-control, and desires and plans to obey the Lord and advance the Kingdom.

---

51 There is somewhat of a debate in Christendom over the usage of "soul" and "spirit." I have chosen the term I believe is most consistent with Scripture. One could switch my usage of "soul" and "spirit" and still benefit from everything I've written here.

With a soul filled with these spiritually good things, the heart provides "output." It powers this man's life to works of worship, love, obedience, sacrifice, courage, and much more.

> *Your heart is not just a pump; it helps with decision-making and choices, acting like a checking station for all the emotions generated by the flow of chemicals from thoughts. In fact, every single cell is connected to your heart and, because your heart responds to and is controlled by your brain, every single cell in your body is affected by your thoughts. Your heart is in constant communication with your brain and the rest of your body, checking the accuracy and integrity of your thought life. As you are about to make a decision, your heart pops in a quiet word of advice. It is well worth listening to this advice, because when you listen to your heart, it secretes the ANF (atrial natriuretic factor)—a hormone produced by the heart that regulates blood pressure and can give you a feeling of peace.*[52]
>
> – Dr. Caroline Leaf, Neurological Pathologist

There is another part of us inside, and that is our spirit. Upon salvation, our spirits are knit to God's Holy Spirit. His voice becomes a part of our life process. When we are led by the Spirit, our spirits receive His direction. The spirit's direction is filtered through our souls, powered by our hearts, and accomplished in our bodies.

Man is created in the image of God. God is a triune being—three Persons in One. Man also has three parts: They are body, soul, and spirit. The Apostle Paul shows us this in his prayer for one of the New Testament churches.

---

52 Leaf, Dr. Caroline. *Switch on Your Brain: The Key to Peak Happiness, Thinking, and Health* (p. 177). Baker Publishing Group, Kindle Edition.

Now may the God of peace himself sanctify you completely, and may your whole spirit and soul and body be kept blameless at the coming of our Lord Jesus Christ. 1 Thessalonians 5:23 (ESV)

Notice the order Paul gives: Spirit, soul, body. Proper life order and good works come from a man who walks in his spirit, which, through salvation, is knit to the Holy Spirit.

Consider this example:

The Spirit directs a man in his spirit to share a word of encouragement with a friend.

The soul processes this word. He may think about the friend: What does he know about this friend? What is the friend going through in this season of life? How does he feel about this friend?

He may think about himself: How can he best deliver this word of encouragement? What will the friend think of him? How have attempts to encourage people gone for him in the past?

He may think about the Lord and pray for additional insight. For example, he may ask himself, are there verses of Scripture he should share?

The body delivers the word. The mouth speaks, the hands gesture, the face gives expression, and even posture and stance play a role.

In this case, the spirit, indwelled by God's Spirit, led the soul, which in turn instructed the body. The person obeyed the leading of the Lord by being in order.

Isaiah 11 describes the Messiah as having the Holy Spirit and then six characteristics or "spirits" of the Spirit. When the Spirit appropriately leads us, our souls are governed by the six other Spirits.

- Our mind should be governed by the Spirit of knowledge.

- Our will should be governed by the Spirit of counsel.

- Our emotions should be governed by the Spirit of might.

- Our memories should be governed by the Spirit of understanding.

- Our imagination should be governed by the Spirit of wisdom.

- Finally, our bodies should live under the Spirit of the Fear of the Lord.

If only it were always this simple!

Sin, Satan, and this world have worked together to hinder this process, and ever since Adam and Eve ate the fruit and disobeyed the Word of the Lord, man has struggled with following the Lord with all of his spirit, soul, and body.

The lost person without Christ has a spirit that is governed by his carnal nature. His soul is corrupt. Envy, jealousy, lust, hatred, and bitterness emanate from it. His body manifests these evil things in violence, sexual perversion, idolatry, and wicked speech.

Other well-meaning followers of Christ try to put the right things in but get the order wrong. They try to listen to the Spirit, but their bodies are in control. A lack of self-discipline leads to unrestrained appetites and silences the voice of the Spirit. Think of those who struggle with addiction. Most of them would be categorized as being led by their bodies. However, in most cases, the body has some self-control (this is the norm in our culture), but the soul leads the person. Some are filled with knowledge, and their minds lead. Others are governed by experience, and their wills lead. Others have passion or pain that puts their emotions in control. In addition, many walk with the painful limps of past traumatic experiences and rejections, and these memories hold a controlling power over them. The spirit is silenced by the continual painful cries of their souls. The imagination has its own tug for control as well. Ambitions, selfish desires, and culturally filtered dreams cause people to work towards goals God never gave them.

You can see how quickly the voices of our inner man can drown out the voice of the Holy Spirit. Culture spends a lot of time emphasizing self-discipline for the body and knowledge, training, and experience for the soul. They provide education for the mind, mentoring for the will, counseling for the emotions, and therapy for the memories. All this, along with things like culture, art, social status, race, and relationships, form the imagination.

If you follow Jesus, you might think church is the solution. Membership and participation in a healthy Body certainly help the spirit find its voice, but many churches fall into the cultural trap of providing only soul ministry. They increase our knowledge, add to our group of mentors, provide counseling, retain therapists on staff, and promote their own arts and agendas while participating in various social programs. However, the sad truth is very few churches do anything to help the spirit communicate with the Holy Spirit and lead the inner man into Christlike wholeness and obedience. Seven times in Revelation, Jesus commanded churches to use their ears to hear what the Holy Spirit is saying. Apparently, it doesn't come to us naturally, even if we are in church.

Because Satan is not a creator but only a counterfeiter, many New Age and worldly practices mimic ministry to the inner man but simply waste time or make matters worse. Many psychological and psychiatric practices are simply humanistic belief systems that teach coping while avoiding Jesus. For example, God created us to dream and, through those dreams, to learn more about ourselves and Him. Men like Sigmund Freud studied dreams and developed extensive insights into our dreams. His insights have shaped the humanistic side of psychiatry and scared most Christians in the Western world from taking any stock in dreams.

We cannot allow the weeds sown by the enemy to keep us from harvesting the wheat of God's provision. Jesus has given us the keys to the Kingdom! We must stop being complacent towards the heart wounds of the people of God and rise up using the power of the Gospel to help them find freedom and healing from years of pain.

To summarize, let's review the problems…

1. An unregenerated spirit

2. A spirit that is saved but not in fellowship with God's Spirit

3. A spirit that is not in control because

    A. The body is in control through unrestrained appetite or…

    B. The soul is in control. The soul can lead through worldliness from cultural influence, error that comes in through lies they believe, heresy, bad experiences or shame, and pain resulting from traumatic experiences, bitterness, relational conflict, or again, shame. In each case, demonization is also a factor to varying degrees.

So, a person needing inner healing needs to be able to hear the Holy Spirit, be self-disciplined in body, and have the lies of worldliness, error, and pain silenced while also having the influence of demons removed.

THE COMMISSION TO HEAL

After demonstrating hundreds of healing miracles, Jesus sent the twelve disciples and later seventy others to go ahead of Him and proclaim His message. While He gave them several instructions, three main tasks stand out. They are to preach that the Kingdom of Heaven is near. They are to heal any sick they encounter while ministering. Lastly, they are to cast devils out of the people they meet. This is the core of inner healing. Preaching the Truth about Jesus and His Kingdom exposes the conflict that goes on not only in this world but inside of us. This is the battle between darkness and light. Inner healing ministry uses the truth of the Gospel to help people see clearly the problematic actions of the enemy in their lives and what Jesus is willing and able to do about those actions. As the disciples preached the message that the Messiah had come, the authorities of this world, demons under the authority of the "prince and power of the air," would manifest. The new Kingdom of Heaven would be revealed in the actions of the apostles who, by their words and Jesus-imparted authority, would command those demons to flee and then immediately see the person who was host to those demons delivered to his right mind. In addition, the effects of sickness and sin in this fallen world were reversed by the preaching of the Gospel and the healing power of Jesus that He had imparted to His followers.

This ministry still continues today. Most people I encounter in a Rapha Room[53] are born again and familiar with the basics of the Gospel and what it promises about a relationship with Jesus and a home in Heaven. However, many of them are ignorant that the Kingdom of Heaven has broken through the enemy lines of darkness, and Jesus has given His church authority to confront lies with Gospel truth, cast out demons, and help the hurting find healing. As you can see, healing and deliverance are tied together. Many people are in physical or emotional pain because demons have been allowed to interfere in their lives and cause torment. Sometimes a demon is confronted and upon being told to leave, the person they left experiences immediate relief or healing. Other times, a lie that the person is believing is confronted with the Gospel, and upon renouncing of that lie and confession of Jesus, they find healing without any demonic activity being noticed.

---

53 Rapha Rooms are the name of a prayer room ministry that I started in 2022. We hold prayer rooms in person and online for individuals all over the world to experience inner healing and spiritual freedom.

> *Many people know intellectually who they are in Christ, but don't experience this in their core. The heart's inability to experience what the head knows is a sure sign of a heart in bondage.*[54]

THE TENDER HEART OF JESUS

In John 4, the story of the Samaritan woman drawing water at a well while encountering Jesus serves as a concise but beautiful picture of inner healing. With simple questions, a patient and tender tone, and a heart of compassion, Jesus reveals Himself to this woman. She is allowed to see Him for who He really is. At the same time, Jesus lets her know that He sees her. He knows of the many mistakes she's made with men, yet He is here to reveal Himself to her. Her encounter with Him transforms her and her entire town. Though, as far as we can tell, this Samaritan experienced no physical healing, she is totally changed from a skeptical, distrusting woman of shame into a passionate evangelist who invites her friends to come meet the man who knows her and loves her just the same.

THE LOCAL CHURCH MINISTRY OF HEALING

James 5 gives us another aspect of inner healing ministry: It is a function of the local church. Confession of sin and acknowledgment of struggles in one's battle against the enemy opens the door for a couple of believers to exhort you with the Gospel. (I see exhortation as a coach telling someone what they already know while they are in the middle of the conflict.) With the exhortation comes healing prayer. This prayer may involve renouncing lies, declaring truth, casting out demons, and praying for physical or emotional healing. In I John 5:13, we are told to confess our sins to the Lord and that He will forgive us and cleanse us. In James 5:16, we're told to confess

---

54 Rustenbach, Rusty. *A Guide for Listening and Inner-Healing Prayer: Meeting God in the Broken Places* (p. 31). The Navigators,, Kindle Edition.

our faults to one another and that we will find healing. Confession to God alone brings cleansing; confession within the Body allows for healing.

MY JOURNEY INTO MINISTERING TO THE INNER MAN

Growing up in church, I was familiar with the miracle of physical healing in the world, but I was pretty ignorant of the idea of inner healing. Many of the people I went to church with continued for decades after salvation, dealing with the effects of bitterness, trauma, sexual dysfunction/perversion, and generational curses. The abundant Christian life found in Jesus didn't seem very abundant. There seemed to be little hope for solutions to their problems. In fact, I have found that many churches develop extensive curriculums that provide nothing more than coping mechanisms and protective measures to help people limp through the "abundant and victorious" Christian life. I'm convinced that some of these curriculums are actually "doctrines of devils" that instill religious performance in people, suppressing the grace of God and diminishing the "now" power of Jesus. They describe godliness without power, but God in me is power. I'm clothed with power, filled with power, imbued with power, and authorized to use it! In other words, to receive inner healing, you must believe in God's power for us today. He speaks to us. He gives us dreams and visions. He uses the Scriptures like weapons and arms us with precisely what we need at just the time we need it. He loves it when three or four people get together just to pray together for the healing of one.

God began to use me in the ministry of inner healing by showing me the pain of my sister-in-law, Amber, and the tender healing touch of Jesus. Amber is one of my wife's best friends. Their parents had six girls, and Candace and Amber are numbers four and five in birth order. Soon after marrying, Candace and I began to spend a good amount of time with Amber and her boyfriend, Matthew Guzzi. We had them over to our house and went on dates with them all over the Chicagoland area. We were with them when Matthew proposed, when they shopped for their first home, and when they found out they were expecting their first child. They had been married for just a few months and Matthew wasn't feeling well. Serious side pain landed him in the hospital. It sounded like appendicitis, and so Candace and I found ourselves sitting in the waiting room keeping Amber company during the surgery. Hours passed. The surgery took much longer than we expected. Finally the surgeon came out and in terms that were a little too technical for my brain, explained that Matthew's appendix was still intact but a large mass had been found and a meeting with a cancer-specialist was of critical importance. I was there in the room when Matthew woke up and was tasked with telling him that there was a much more serious health issue than had been previously suspected.

Life for the two newlyweds radically changed. Trips to the Mayo Clinic, chemotherapy, radiation, more surgeries…

The stress of the situation led to a miscarriage.

Eighteen months later in 2010, at the age of 23, Matthew passed away.

As years passed and Amber rebuilt her life, another Matthew caught Amber's attention. Matt Turner had overcome drug addiction through the power of Jesus and built a successful real estate business. In 2012, they married, and in 2015, they welcomed their first child. Amber's life was filled with new joy and excitement. Still, her grief was present, just under the surface of her emotions. Her nerves were raw and any sort of health struggles or mild concerns could send her into depression and anxiety.

As God brought me deeper in fellowship with His Holy Spirit, I became convinced that the wounds of grief that Amber was feeling could be healed by Jesus. She had been in counseling, gone through therapy, been faithful to church, and continued in regular devoted time with the Lord through prayer and Bible reading, yet the wounds of her heart clearly remained open. In 2020, I found myself on the phone with her. She had called Candace distraught, and Candace had put her phone on speaker and invited me into the conversation. In this latest season of anxiety, Amber found herself crippled by the fear that her oldest daughter, Eden, would succumb to an untimely death. The tension in Amber's voice was obvious as she described to me the torment she was experiencing both while sleeping and during the day. She kept Eden close but was exhausted with the constant paranoia she felt. As she shared her pain, Candace and I began to pray. During my prayer, the Lord showed me a wall. He showed me that Amber's unresolved grief had caused Amber to separate herself from the Lord. She felt like God couldn't be trusted. She'd lost her first love, lost her first child, and had to start all over again. And no matter how good life was now, the pain of those losses had convinced her that God was a God who hurts people, and He was bound to do it again.

Saying nothing of this vision, I began to share the Gospel with Amber. This probably seemed ridiculous to her. After all, she was just a year younger than me, and we had gone to the same school and church all of our lives. We both knew the Gospel inside out. We had personally led dozens of people to the Lord on our own. Yet, at that moment, in a battle for her mind and her faith, fighting against the bullying tactics of Satan, the accuser, she had lost perspective. I've been there. The pain can feel so deep, the darkness so heavy, that the love and light of God feel like an illusion. That's when a Word is needed. A prayerful brother and sister need to be the voices of that light and love.

I told Amber that the Father loved her more than she could imagine. I told her that He was a Redeemer and a Friend. I told her that He was enjoying this season of life with her and wasn't planning on snatching it from her. I told her that He wanted to heal her pain and grief and would do just that if she would give it to Him. I asked her to close her eyes. "Can you picture Jesus?" I asked.

"All I can see is a wall," she responded.

I was surprised, to say the least. She was seeing the same thing that the Lord had just shown me! I was excited but still unsure of what to do next, so I prayed again. The Lord told me that the wall needed to be broken down by the one who had built it. I felt in my spirit that He was telling me that Amber had built a barrier in her spiritual life to protect her from Him since she believed He was the ultimate cause of all of her pain. I spent some time reaffirming His tenderness and love for her. I quoted Scriptures. I prayed with her. Then I asked her if she trusted the Lord enough to tear down this wall.

With her eyes closed and tears streaming down her face, sitting in a dark bedroom, overcome with depression, a born-again girl gave herself to Jesus in the strangest of ways. She set the phone down and began swinging her arms in a physical act of submission, tearing down this wall she sensed in the spirit. Candace and I listened and just kept praying.

Suddenly I heard her gasp. The weeping of sorrow and depression shifted and she wept for several minutes tears of surprise and joy. Finally after gaining some composure, she shared the vision that God gave her as she tore down the wall.

I approached the wall in my spirit, afraid of what I'd find on the other side. I so desperately wanted to be healed from my grief but I had such fear that God would hurt me again. I swung my arm at the wall and a door-sized hole opened up. Through that opening, came Jesus. He held me, told me He loved me. Then He took my hand and led me through the door. There, on the other side, stood my daughter. He showed me that I had built a barrier not only from him but from her as well. This fear I had of losing her had caused me to distance myself emotionally not just from Him but also from my daughter. But He had been caring for her the whole time. And now that I had given Him my pain, and let go of my fear, I could come out from this safety barrier I had built and live in the joy of His Presence while loving my daughter deeply without fear."

Beautiful…Jesus heals broken hearts. Hallelujah! Jesus is wonderful.

Years later, Amber is an intercessor who often spends hours weeping at the feet of Jesus in the Spirit, praying for the hurting and listening on behalf of those who are doing inner healing ministry. Her depression is gone. She knows she is safe with Jesus. Just a couple of hours of praying and an encounter with Jesus will do that.

I've seen hundreds of people have experiences like Amber's in the years since. I've seen crazy visions that led to miraculous deliverances from addiction. I've laid my hands on the shoulders of people and felt their burdens lift off their backs. Decades-old wounds of abuse, neglect, rejection, hatred, paranoia, and grief, to name a few, all lifted during a time of prayer. A brother, a sister, a son or daughter of God, encountering Jesus like it's the first time, and finding the healing that only He can give.

In 2022, after holding dozens of sessions in person and over the phone and seeing God do countless miracles of healing broken hearts, I launched a ministry called Rapha Rooms. I've sat with individuals from dozens of churches who felt like they were in darkness. I've prayed for them, asked them simple questions, and invited Jesus to do what He wants. He never disappoints. Words cannot express the depth of the kindness of Jesus. He always shows up and affirms the love of Abba Father.

Do you need inner healing? Have people walked out on you? Do the critical labels of unkind words spoken in the past still linger and torment you in your present? Do you feel or hear the voice of shame? Has sexual sin, grief, or fear left marks on your soul?

Do you see recurring patterns in your life? Perhaps you get close to someone and then lose them only to start the process all over again with someone else. Perhaps you move from church to church every couple of years. Perhaps there's a deep brokenness that lies unresolved in the depths of your heart.

Jesus loves to heal broken hearts. Let it begin today.

Father, I ask you to begin the healing process for my friend who is reading this. You're close to the brokenhearted and don't intend to leave them this way. Would you begin to uproot the toxic trees in their spirits that bear the awful fruits that they are experiencing, and would you plant truth, love, and hope in the gardens of their souls? Let the truths of the Gospel of King Jesus wash over them in fresh ways and overwhelm them with your kindness and strength.

Amen

CHAPTER 8

FORGIVENESS

On the journey of discovering more about the Holy Spirit, I never expected that forgiveness would be such a major factor. I was hungry for God's power, hungry to experience His Presence like never before, hungry to see Him work, and I kept telling Him I was willing to do anything in order to receive these things. His response to me was to release.

When I was seven years old, I found myself kneeling on the steps of a platform in a small church in Greenville, Michigan. My dad had just preached a sermon on being a follower of Jesus. Our family of four had all traveled together to this meeting to hear my dad preach a message in an evening service. It was February, and I remember it being very cold.

As the sermon progressed, I remember beginning to cry. God's Spirit was touching me. It was a feeling I had not experienced before. Something deep inside of me was breaking open, and for the duration of the message, tears flowed freely from my eyes. I had no language for it, and I'm not sure my Baptist family did either. "You have a tender heart," Was their main explanation.

But this was more than just being sensitive. Something was shifting inside of me. God spoke to me, not through an audible voice or mental impression. He was speaking to me through tears. Long before someone ever learns to speak in tongues, I believe they learn to speak to the Lord in tears. Before seeing a Resurrected Jesus, Peter wept bitterly over his denial of Christ. Before she would conceive Samuel, Hannah wept bitterly, and the Lord gave her the desire of her heart. Before the Cross, Jesus wept in a Garden.

I have found that when God uses our tears, He uses them for five primary purposes.

- To open our spiritual ears to a Word He has for us.
- To water the soil of something He wants to grow.
- To wash our hearts from the pain of our mistakes.
- To prepare our hearts to fulfill the heavy calling ahead of us.
- To open our hearts to the anguish that another person is feeling in a Spirit of intercession.

At the conclusion of my dad's sermon, I went forward during prayer and knelt on the steps along with many others. The message had been powerful, and the whole room seemed deeply moved. As I continued weeping, I heard my dad speak over the sound of many people praying. "I feel tonight that God is calling someone to preach."

As I heard the words, I knew why I'd been crying. God had been speaking to me. He was asking me to dedicate my life to Him, and so I did.

My dad grew up in Michigan. The son of a hard-working, self-made, and successful couple with conservative Midwestern values, he always walked with the confidence of a man who knew he could work hard and succeed at anything he put his mind to. Church played a major role in his life. My grandfather and namesake, Ken Schaap, and three other families started a church in Holland, a suburb of Grand Rapids, Michigan. No one in the group was ordained, so they searched for and found a pastor. They scrabbled together some money to give him a salary, and soon, the Rose Park Baptist Church was officially birthed. Sixty-three years and eight pastors later, my Grandfather is approaching 90 years of age. I recently sat with him in his typical spot, third row, left side of the auditorium. Tears trickled down his eyes during the service. He loves Jesus as much as ever.

Believing he would always work with his father in construction and real estate, my dad was surprised by God when an evangelist came to town and held a citywide revival. The services broke something in my dad's spirit, and after a night of prayer, he surrendered to a call. He was going to be a preacher.

He left for Bible college, winding up at Hyles-Anderson College under the leadership of the most influential Baptist pastor in America, Dr. Jack Hyles. His youngest daughter, Cindy, caught my dad's eye, and soon they were married. My sister Jaclynn was born within a few years, and three years later, I came along.

Dad was the Vice President of the college and a much sought-after speaker, preaching in dozens of churches around America each year. Though he was incredibly gifted with charisma and the talent to lead, he was also a great dad to my sister and me. He became my hero. He wasn't just my hero but the hero of hundreds of young people around the country. His passion for God, outgoing personality, and kindness to everyone he met caused him to have a massive following. It was pretty fun as a boy to have a dad who always noticed me while at the same time being the hero of nearly everyone around him.

Dad authentically loved Jesus. I caught him more than once, on his face in passionate prayer, tears soaking the ground around him. I saw him crawl out of bed in the middle of the night to help someone in crisis. Though we weren't wealthy, I remember many times when we would buy several bags of groceries and deliver them to the homes of single parents or people who'd just lost their jobs. Without fanfare, he raised thousands of dollars to put dozens of children into private school, purchasing their shoes, clothing, and school supplies. Often he would take a side job or two, pouring concrete on his own to pay for their tuition.

Dad loved our family. The marriage I saw in our home was a happy one. I remember arguments and challenging times, but they were few and far between compared to the genuine love I experienced and the hundreds of good memories. As I grew older and fell in love with Candace, it made perfect sense when I told my dad at my bachelor party that I wanted a marriage just like the one I'd seen him have with my mom.

When I was 16, my grandfather passed away, and the church voted my dad in as pastor. Suddenly, he was leading a congregation with 20,000 active members, a college with nearly 2,000 students, a network of churches numbering in the thousands, and a movement of hundreds of thousands of conservative Christians. At that time, a network of approximately 15,000 independent Baptist churches loosely fellowshipped together because of their shared values. Several colleges of various sizes competed for students in this unofficial denomination, and now, my father was one of the leading influencers of this movement.

I could tell he felt the pressure, but I watched with pride as he applied his incredible work ethic to moving this ministry into the 21st century. With fresh energy and fresh vision, the church grew. A new auditorium was built with a seating capacity of 7,500. Momentum continued.

I was following in his footsteps. Though I did not have the same measure of influence, I still did my share of traveling and speaking. Eventually, I became a Vice President at the college, overseeing the academics and preparing to overhaul the training process to position a new generation to lead Baptist churches in America. I was ambitious and proud to be in such a position at a relatively young age. I was excited. I was not only in the family, but now I had been given a position in the inner circle of leaders in a massive and influential ministry. I felt a sense of destiny. I was the third generation and would build a lasting legacy upon a great foundation.

By that time, the ministry was having what I thought were growing pains. The 2008 economic downturn had hit the ministry hard and caused a round of layoffs. Criticism from other leaders came. I saw it as jealousy and a grab for power. I was defensive of what we were doing and frustrated by those unwilling to look to the future.

For the first time, I saw my dad as less than my hero. He seemed to be cracking under the pressure. Behind closed doors, he increasingly used anger and profanity to get his point across. In family gatherings, he spoke occasionally of resigning. Our family trips became more lavish, but an underlying current of stress and frustration seemed to accompany them.

I knew that Dad was struggling with both his physical and mental health. I did not suspect at all that he was in the middle of infidelity or, worse, criminal behavior. On a Thursday in July, sitting on a platform in front of nearly 7,000 teenagers, I received a message asking me to go to my mom's office. I was told that a staff member had evidence that my dad had gotten involved with a teenage girl that he had been counseling.

That night, I confronted him.

My hero looked cornered. His words were angry and hurtful. He refused to sit down with me and explain. He lied to me. Then he stormed off. That was the night my hero and dad broke my heart.

An hour later, I sat with church leadership and told them everything I knew. An investigation ensued. Unbeknownst to me, the Sheriff was called, and then the FBI. I was naively hopeful that something could be done to restore Dad. I knew only a tiny percentage of what had actually happened and, as a family member, was understandably left out of the loop. Less than a week later, my dad called my phone.

Ken,

The church board chairman called me and fired me about an hour ago. For most of the time you've known me, I've been the man you thought I was. However, recently, I've been a terribly immoral man. I'm under investigation by the authorities. I'm not sure what will happen. I'm so sorry. I wish this would have never happened. I love you, Son

I'm not the only one to get news like this. Some get it much earlier in life. I cried with three children recently who had just found out that their dad didn't "love their mom anymore." Not knowing or willing to help the kids process their shock, he'd sent them to church so that Pastor Ken and Candace could help them process the news. Watching them weep, and then argue with each other, and then weep some more, I was reminded of how lucky I'd been not to have had that kind of disappointment until I was well in my 20s. So many others live with disappointment and brokenness as a part of their lives from when their memories start to form.

Neurologists tell us we process painful memories throughout our bodies. Cells that hold memories are found in the human brain, the heart, and our stomachs. Even some heart transplant patients have found after their surgeries that they have new memories and tastes. Images and emotions from the past come from a life they've never lived, their new heart reminding them that it once beat in the chest of another soul. The painful events of life leave their mark in all three areas. The mind struggles to process, the heart aches with disappointment, and the gut clenches with a deep fear of what this means for the future.

If you've walked this earth for any length of time, you've probably experienced this: words or actions that are so painful that they affect your entire body. Pain like this is not experienced in a vacuum. It comes from somebody. A person or group of people take action or speak words that shock your system and leave you struggling to catch your breath, maintain your composure, or—in the most egregious of cases—to survive.

One of the great ministry opportunities that I've been privileged to start and help lead is the "Rapha Room Ministry" in local churches like The Father's House. A Rapha Room is a two-hour session of prayer, deliverance, and inner healing ministry that a team of two or three individuals leads with a client. Of the hundreds I've been a part of, I haven't had one yet where there wasn't some deep pain at the root of their struggle. They range from the rejection of a parent, abuse from someone they trusted, or a marriage that ended in hostility. Recently, I sat with a bodybuilder and veteran of the United States military. His wife had dragged him to our church in search of help. We waited in my office while his wife went through her Rapha Room. He told me she needed it badly. Sensing there was more, I asked him if he wanted to talk. "No," he said. "I'm here for my wife. I'm doing great. She's the one who needs the help."

"I understand," I said. "Would you mind if I asked you a few questions while we wait?"

"I guess."

I asked him some basic questions about his background and the type of home he was raised in. Then I asked him when his sexual awakening had happened.

"When I was seven. A teenage friend of my sister took me into a room and taught me everything. I've been sexually active ever since."

The details he gave of things that had happened afterward were disturbing and heartbreaking. He shared them with a practiced look of toughness. Arms crossed, back tensed, displaying that posture of one who has survived some things and wants you to know it's had no effect.

I met his gaze and said, "I'm sorry. That should have never happened. No one is meant to go through something like that at seven."

He wasn't expecting that. Tremors involuntarily came deep from his gut. Pain locked away for decades rocketed to the surface. Tears shot from his eyes before he could get his hands in front of his face to conceal them. He wept in front of me, his entire body in conflict with his soul, until he finally gave in, laid his head on my desk, and cried for ten straight minutes, neither of us saying a word.

God did significant healing in his heart that day, but I've never seen pain manifest in a person's entire body like that. He'd never been allowed to safely process all the trauma that he had experienced in his life. One simple question unlocked it. One sentence of compassion opened the door to it.

I've been on the other side of the table. I've been the one who was broken by a question. Within a few months of starting the church, we were struggling. Finances had dried up, health struggles were worsening, and the community's response to our church was apathetic. I was discouraged. I had moved with my friends with a dream, and now it seemed like a nightmare. One day, I arrived at the church office to a note. Our sign had been damaged in a storm a couple of weeks earlier, and we lacked the money to repair it. It gave our church the appearance of being out of business. The note was anonymous. As best as I can recall, it read…

"Looks like you won't be here much longer. I knew you'd fail. Take your family back to where you came from. You were never wanted here. Good riddance."

I should have let it motivate me and seen it as the devil overplaying his hand, but it was another of many notes I'd received that month. My dad was finishing his first year of a 12-year prison sentence, and our relationship had grown contentious. The shock of everything that had happened had worn off, and he was just angry. He began writing letters, each one more angry than the last. He felt I had broken the family's trust by turning him in to the leadership, and he wanted me to know he would never forgive me.

On top of that, he didn't believe I could pastor a church. If I didn't know how to treat my own father in his time of need, how could I ever expect to help anyone who was hurting or in need? I was nothing without him. I had done nothing without him. I would fail, and the church would fail.

The words stung so deeply. I could feel them in my body, and as I stood at the door holding an anonymous taunt from some stranger, I realized I believed it. I was a failure. This church was going to fail. I had been wrong.

A few minutes after walking into my office, I heard a knock. An older gentleman came in, introducing himself as the pastor of a church down the street from us. He asked me who I was, and I shared a brief story of how we'd gotten there. Tears filled his eyes.

"You've been through a lot, son. It's amazing that you're still standing and pursuing Jesus. For what it's worth, I'm proud of you and excited about what God is going to do through you and this church. I'm here to help in any way I can. This community desperately needs you and the Gospel."

Then he stood up, hugged me, and left. Managing to hold it in until he walked out the door, I lay down in our little church auditorium and let the waves of pain escape through tears. I felt seen by God. He'd sent me someone to love me and help me process the pain. My earthly father was done with me. God was my Father now, and would never turn away from me.

Jesus came to earth for a lot of reasons. I believe a primary one was to help us with our pain. The preacher in Hebrews says, He was touched with the feeling of our infirmities, tempted in every way we were, and is now qualified to intercede for us as our High Priest before the Father. Jesus couldn't be an Intercessor until He felt what it was like to hurt like us. Isaiah said that the Lord would carry our grief and sorrow upon Himself. Jesus knows pain.

HE FELT THE SORROW OF OUR GRIEF

Jesus understands the pain of loss. He grieved with His disciples when His cousin, John the Baptist, died. He wept greatly at the home of Lazarus in sorrow over his death. No one ever loved as deeply as Jesus because no one ever had a heart as pure as Jesus. The deeper you love, the more love can hurt. When you understand this, you begin to see a different side to the powerful love of God. His love opens Him up to pain.

Since Adam left Eden, God has watched the people He loves walk away. By the time you get to the prophets in your Bible reading, you see a God who almost seems weary of hurting. Anguish pours from the pages as He speaks of the betrayal He feels from the unfaithfulness and idolatry that His people have shown Him.[55] The Mighty Creator, Yahweh, takes His heart and places it in the shell of humanity. A human body with a divine heartbeat, the mystery of the God-Man Jesus. Jesus is subjected to pain and loss. "He is acquainted with grief," the King James Version says, an eloquent way of saying that God knows what it's like to lose.

How can the Creator, all-powerful and all-knowing, lose? Because He loves us. He gave up control of us so that He could enjoy the pleasure found in being chosen, but with that comes the sting of loss. It wasn't too long into this experiment called Creation before He was peering over Adam's shoulder, no doubt weeping with him as he looked on the dead body of Abel. This was the first actual cost of the Fall. The fruit had led to a banishment and a sentence, but the real cost lay here, clutched to the breasts of a tormented mother. Eve held the corpse of her son, his body beaten and bloodied with the violence of a jealous soul. By Genesis 6, the earth is "filled with violence," and God repents of ever making man. "Why did I ever do this?" seems to be the cry of a God with a pure heart who made a people that had fallen into perversion and chaos. God understands grief. Every soul that slipped beneath the flood waters was someone that He loved. His familiarity with grief bursts out in an exclamation of "Stop!" Abraham stood over his son with a knife poised to kill, preparing an amazing picture of resurrection, but the Father of Heaven provided a better plan. A Lamb would die. God understands grief. He stood watching from the throne room of Heaven as His only begotten Son wept in exceeding sorrow, the spirit of death hovering over Him. "Let this cup pass from me!" he cried with a loud voice. The Father said nothing. Hours would pass, and soon the Son would hang from a cross, unrecognizable as a man, mangled from the brutality of Satan-possessed soldiers. "My God, why have you forsaken me?" He cries again.

---

55 One example of many is found in Hosea 6:6-7 *I want you to show love, not offer sacrifices. I want you to know me more than I want burnt offerings. But like Adam, you broke my covenant and betrayed my trust.*

The Father turns His back, and with it, darkness covers Calvary in the afternoon hours.

God understands grief.

JESUS FELT THE STING OF OUR GRIEVANCES

"He turned His back to the smiters," Isaiah wrote. God understands what it's like to be offended. Not only can the Creator lose, the Creator can suffer. No man has ever been filled with joy and hope like Jesus, yet no man has ever carried more rejection. "He came unto His own, and His own received Him not."

"Foxes have their holes and birds their nests, but the Son of man has no place to lay His head." He was born in a borrowed manger designed for animals and died in a borrowed tomb not fit for the King of kings. In between, His identity was questioned, His miracles were dismissed, and His followers turned away or, worse, sold Him out for worthless land. He was scorned, criticized, mocked, spat upon, beaten with rods, and torn with whips. He, the Son of God, was traded for an anarchist thief, Bar-Abba, "the son of the father." He was crushed, bruised, pierced, murdered! His final minutes were spent in naked humiliation as his mother looked on. His possessions were dispatched through gambling, and his thirst was met with the taste of sour retribution. His only response?

"Father, forgive them."

JESUS FELT THE PAIN OF OUR GUILT

"The Lord hath laid on Him the iniquities of us all."

I can still remember how I felt the first time I looked at pornography without my wife knowing. I remember how I felt when I stole money in desperation from a friend who had entrusted me with it. I remember how I felt when I lied to get out of trouble as a high-school student. I remember how I felt when I received the foreclosure notice on the front door of my home, unable to provide for my family. Each action of deceit and darkness seemed to take away a bit of my soul. It left me in shock, feeling the anxious weight of despair and dread. Sin has an awful bite. I can't imagine what the shock of experiencing our sin felt like to the Holy One as He agonized in the Garden. Gethsemane is the oil press, the place of crushing, and the weight of humanity's sin fell on the Son and crushed Him, His pure mind crushed with the agony of an infinite number of perversions, the Gentle Shepherd exposed to the pain of endless abuses. The effects of child abuse, infanticide, murders, rape, and all the evil done in darkness poured out on the Son of Man. Neurologists have discovered only recently the science behind what toxic thoughts do to a person's body. The shock of all sin laid on Him in a moment aged the Son a lifetime, breaking His heart in such a way that when the time came, He simply released Himself. "Father, into thy hands, I commend my Spirit." Giving up the ghost, God the Giver of life, paid for our guilt and died.

THE FORGIVENESS OF JESUS

"Have you forgiven him?" a friend asked.

"Of course I have!" I responded indignantly.

My friend was not convinced, but said nothing.

I was sitting in the cab of a box truck driving through the mountains of southern Alaska. I had shared the entire story of my dad's scandal with a pastor friend. We had finished a week of teen camp. He had hosted, and I had preached. We were headed to town, where I would preach for the Sunday services at his church. After all that I had said, his question seemed out of place. Hadn't he heard of all the terrible things my dad had done, of all the ways he had hurt me and so many others? Why would he ask me to forgive? None of this mess was my fault.

Deep down, I heard a little whisper in my spirit and knew he was right. I needed to forgive. So naturally, the first thing I did was buy a book.

R.T. Kendall is a retired pastor. Born in Ashland, Kentucky, he eventually went to Cambridge and studied theology before becoming the pastor of Westminster Chapel in London, England. He has written over 50 books, but his most famous work is *Total Forgiveness*. Reading his book produced another holy moment for me. I saw the beauty of the Gospel and the heavy responsibility that came with it. The Gospel is the power of God unto salvation. It is a seed that bears the fruit of eternal life in us. One of those fruits is forgiveness. The Apostle Paul wrote, "Be kind to one another, tenderhearted, forgiving one another, as God in Christ forgave you."[56] The God who forgave us has called us to forgive others.

On the surface, the doctrine of forgiveness is a beautiful, poignant theological truth. In real life, it can be a terrifying challenge. We learn to hold onto our pain, nursing our wounds, and treating our emotions with a thousand coping mechanisms. The enemy convinces us that we deserve this. We were wronged, and our pain has earned us the right to hold onto it. We hold grudges, join other wounded souls, and soon find identity in our pain. The pain we hold becomes the fuel to our anger. We stay angry because we keep hurting, and our wounds soon become infected.

Our world is filled with infected pain. The Bible calls it bitterness. It's a toxic tree that bears deadly fruit. Race riots, wars, murders, abuses, and a million nasty words spoken on a daily basis all make this world a darker place, the fruits of a forest of bitter trees. To combat this, Jesus hung on a tree of forgiveness, and through it, He calls us to take up our own crosses of wounds, rejections, and betrayals and to follow Him.

Forgiving my father came to a head unexpectedly on a February evening in 2021. Candace and I had put the kids to bed and were standing in our living room watching worship music videos on YouTube on our television and praying. She walked over to me, brushed some oil on my forehead, and began to pray over me. She held me close, praying in my ear,

---

56 Ephesians 4:32.

asking the Holy Spirit to renew me and heal any brokenness in my heart. She had done this for me several times before, but God, in His wisdom, had something special for me that night. As she prayed, my legs began to tremble until I lay down on the floor. Candace knelt next to me and continued praying. Deep tremors began to rise in my stomach, and I began to shake uncontrollably. I had never experienced anything like it. Feeling safe with my wife, knowing that she was familiar with the sometimes strange effects that the Presence of God can have, I relaxed and let the Lord have His way. I shook for nearly 2 hours. As I shook, I had a vision.

In the Spirit, I saw a giant mountain off in the distance, and as I looked, I heard the noise of an engine and turned to see a motorcycle headed my way. I realized I was standing beside a road with greenery all around me. The motorcycle that pulled up was an older bike. It looked like a Harley-Davidson from the 1930s. The rider was an older man wearing a leather bomber jacket. I got on the bike behind him, and he drove me to a large metal barn. Going inside, he led me to a scarred work table covered with leather pieces. I knew in this moment that this man was a picture of God the Father to me, and in realizing it, I began to weep. He was making me a jacket. It was a brown leather one, just like His. I watched Him give attention to detail after detail until, finally finished, He stepped behind me and helped me put it on. It fit perfectly. I felt in this moment a warmth of love like I'd never known before. I was seen and known by my Heavenly Father. What an incredible gift! Just as this thought entered my mind, I thought of my dad. "Abba, how do you feel about my dad? Will he be coming with us?" I asked. The answer came in the sound of another motorcycle. Abba led me out the barn door in time to see another motorcycle pulling up. On the front was a man that could only be Jesus. His face was filled with love for me, and His smile seemed to brighten our entire plateau. Behind Him sat my dad. A huge smile crossed his face as he saw me and waved. Then, together, they rode off. I looked at Abba Father. He smiled at me and led me back inside. Though He spoke no words, I knew that He would care for my dad and that it was time to release him to Jesus.

When I came out of the vision, I was pretty shaken. The Lord had called me to forgive my father, and so there on the floor of my living room, I released all the pain and anguish I had felt towards him to Jesus.

Years before, when I was a teenager, my dad had promised that as a gift for high school graduation, he would rent some motorcycles and take me on a road trip out West. Shortly after, he became the senior pastor, and the schedule of his new responsibilities kept him extremely busy. Though we did several special things together, that motorcycle trip never happened. It wasn't a big deal. I'd forgotten about it. My wife didn't even know about it. But God chose a motorcycle vision to help me forgive my dad.

On May 4, 2022, I sat in my truck outside a medium-security federal prison in Ashland, Kentucky. I watched a man walk out the front door carrying a cardboard box of possessions. He wore a cheap prison-issue light gray cotton jogging suit. His shoes were cheap tennis shoes with a lot of steps on them. I'm sure it was one of the most stressful walks of his life. Would they let him get all the way to the car? He got in the back seat of my truck, and along with my sister, we drove away. We went to Starbucks, and he opened a duffel bag of things I had surprised him with. The first thing he opened was a watch. It was just a $50 item I'd bought on Amazon. It symbolized a lot more than that. Before he could put it on his wrist, he began to weep. I choked back tears in the drive-thru. "I love you, Son," he said.

"I love you too, Pa."

Many still suffer today from the fallout of all that happened at my home church. The name at the center of all that pain is my dad's. A sex crime committed by a megachurch pastor makes ripples in a community and church movement that only God can resolve. There are people who have been hurt much more than I was, victims who carry deep wounds that a prison sentence for the culprit doesn't do nearly enough to heal. The American justice system doesn't heal wounds. Even when a man is brought to justice, it never seems like enough for victims who lost their innocence or for families that are trying to help pick up the pieces.

This call for forgiveness is not a call I make lightly. It's not a call personally for my dad. It's a call from a God who knows pain to a world that needs His help in finding relief from theirs. The message of forgiveness is as offensive today as it was 2,000 years ago. "Take up your cross" was a phrase that triggered a lot of hurting people. Having endured seeing many a son, brother, or father brutalized under Roman rule by being nailed to a rugged intersection of wood, the Jews would have been pretty sensitive towards a Rabbi asking them to each pick up their own crosses and follow Him. Jesus knew what He was asking. He would soon carry one of misery and agony that no other person could ever lift. He could have come down, could have called thousands of angels to rescue Him, but He stayed until *it was finished.* Are you willing to carry yours? Knowing that compared to His, it is a far lighter load and a far shorter duration through which you must carry it? Will you take up your cross and forgive?

So, how do we forgive and answer the thousands of questions and concerns that pop up when we even consider it? We live in a world of injustice, cover-ups, abuse, manipulation, and inequality. Isn't Biblical forgiveness too simple a concept for our day?

Here's what I've discovered. I've developed a simple acronym, "P-A-R-T-E-D" to help you begin to move on from your pain.

1. Partner with a trusted person or team of people.
2. Acknowledge your pain.
3. Release your anger.
4. Transfer your right to get even.
5. Express Forgiveness.
6. Declare Blessings.

PARTNER WITH A PERSON OR TEAM OF PEOPLE

Healing takes purpose. If you're going to heal, you need help and direction. One of the greatest functions of the Body of Christ is its ability to heal itself. Those who are hurting can find healing from healthy people within the Body. You need a team, a "one another" of people that can help you bear your burden. The deeper the pain, the more qualified the individuals may need to be that you choose. Holding the pain inside and not talking about it is a recipe for disaster. It is a wound of the soul that can become infected unless treated properly. In the case of minor offenses caused by a friend, I seek them out and work through reconciliation. In other minor cases, I process it with my wife or a close friend before releasing it to the Lord. Other more intense seasons of life have been processed with a prayer team from my church or another trusted ministry. Certainly therapy and counseling can also play a role in the healing process.

ACKNOWLEDGE THE PAIN THEY CAUSED YOU

People who have been hurt in a life-altering way tend to talk about it until it's been dealt with. R.T. Kendall says that you know a person hasn't fully forgiven someone if they're always bringing up how they were hurt. Once you've found someone to sit down with, it's important to inventory the pain that the perpetrator has caused you. This is a principle found in Scripture. As you read through the Old Testament Law, you'll discover dozens of instructions for how to deal with specific violations of the Law. While Jesus paid for all our sins on the Cross, the principle of accounting remains the same. It's important for us to speak out about the ways we were hurt. Often when I am helping a client or church member, I jot down a list of categories. The day of my writing this chapter began with a two-hour Rapha Room with a lady in her 50s who was hurt years before by an unfaithful husband. With her help, I made a list of seven ways that this man's actions hurt her. He made her feel abandoned, unsafe, unloved, unattractive, like a failure, shamed, and foolish. As I led her through a prayer of forgiveness, I made sure to have her mention each of these feelings to the Lord. The act of speaking them out, removed the power that these wounds have held over her all these years.

RELEASE YOUR ANGER

When someone hurts us, it is natural and common for us to harbor anger towards them for what they have done. This anger is like the gallon of milk that my kids leave out after pouring their cereal. It spoils fast. Spoiled anger is bitterness, a toxic emotion that opens us up to Satan's strategies and suggestions. Often I'll have the client close their eyes and imagine bringing a box containing all of their anger and rage related to the offender to the foot of the cross. In some cases, this erases all anger immediately. In others, it begins a process of release that leads to complete healing over time.

TRANSFER YOUR RIGHT TO GET EVEN

The Kingdom of God contains several rights and agreements. When someone offends us, we tend to emotionally grab on to vengeance and hold it closely in hopes of one day repaying them for the hurt they've caused us. The act of forgiveness brings us to the One who hung on a cross for us, carrying our shame and experiencing all of our pain on our behalf while also atoning for our sins and rejection that we directed at God. Many who suffer in constant emotional torment do so not just because of untreated wounds but because of unreleased anger. The release brings relief.

EXPRESS FORGIVENESS

While there aren't any magic words in prayer, the words "Jesus, I forgive…" come pretty close. So many times in my life, a deep churning of anguish in my heart has totally disappeared with these simple words. Forgiveness and reconciliation are two different things. We forgive someone *to* Jesus. His suffering for the pain of all mankind makes Him the Gatekeeper of relational and emotional healing. By going to Him and declaring forgiveness, we enter into His heart and find everything we need for healing and strength.

DECLARE BLESSINGS

Bless those who curse you. Pray for those who hurt you. (Luke 6:28, NLT)

When we treat everyone as an image-bearer of God, made as a part of His Divine plan, we enter into a deeper level of understanding with the Lord. Blessing people because they are God's Creation, *regardless* of what they've done to us, reveals humility in us. It is perhaps the most Christ-like prayer we can pray. *"Father, forgive them. They know not what they do."*

One of the most life-changing steps in my prayer life began when I heard John Bevere preach on "The Bait of Satan." In it, he challenged the listeners to pray for their enemies the way they would pray for themselves. As I've taken a list of my personal desires and prayed it over my critics, I've felt the waves of Abba's love wash over me in steadily increasing powerful measures.

"IT'S TOO SIMPLE"

I get this a lot. Counselors, therapists, medical experts, and victim advocates each have their opinions and processes for what healing should look like. Each of those fields is important and I have great respect for the individuals who treat the hurting. My challenge for each hurting person is to look to Jesus and consider what He can do. The Kingdom of God is more amazing than many people in these fields give credit. A simple sinner's prayer can make an eternal difference between Heaven and Hell, and a simple forgiveness prayer can transform a hurting soul into one filled with hope. I've seen it hundreds of times. Jesus is still healing the hurting through the power of forgiveness.

PRAYER FOR FORGIVENESS

Jesus, I come to you in order to forgive _____ *for the ways they have hurt me. Their actions towards me have caused me to feel* _____
_____. *I take all the anger and pain that they have caused me and give it to you, Jesus.*

I release my right to get even with _____ *and to continually tell people about how they have wronged me.*

I forgive _____ *completely with your help, Jesus, just as You have forgiven me.*

I bless _____ *with all the blessings that I would want if I were them. Bless their relationships, their finances, and their health.*

Jesus, thank you for your healing touch in my soul.

Amen

CHAPTER 9

DREAMS

I found myself walking down a hall lined with doors. The hallway reminded me almost of an airport terminal or large conference center. Each door I looked at was closed, but I knew in my spirit that each was unlocked and available to me. Behind each door was a church of some sort. I knew this is as a part of the dream, though I only ended up opening one. I proceeded forward to the edge of the hall and walked through the door straight ahead. (There may have been two doors at the end, so I chose the left.)

When I entered the door, I found myself in an auditorium with seating arranged in square rows. There were at least four of these square sections. I sat in the back of the rear-right square facing the front of the room. As I waited for the service to start, two men sat next to me. I was on the end of the row, so they squeezed by me and, after doing so, motioned to me to "pass the crackers." At the edge of my row, I noticed a saucer plate of cheddar crackers. I took one and passed it down. After passing it, I noticed another plate of light-colored crackers. They were thicker than normal. I took one and passed it down to the men on my right. This time, they looked at me disapprovingly, at which time I realized that these were communion crackers.

The service began shortly, and after a time of music, the leader of the service came out. I thought him to be the pastor at first, dressed in costume.

He wore a white robe and was going from seat to seat, administering communion. I could not see what he was doing with each person but suddenly realized that the cracker I had taken for communion was missing. I found myself squirming, looking for it. As soon as I found it, I realized the pastor was standing in front of me. His hair was dark and cut short. He was light-complexioned and of average height. His hands were strong, and the robe he wore looked like it had been made for him. He didn't seem like a man in costume but rather like he was wearing a regular outfit. His eyes were the most unforgettable part of his appearance. I've never seen eyes like this. They were normal enough, brown in color if I remember right, but they burned with a clear mixture of love, passion, sorrow, and burden. I could feel in his gaze that he felt all of these things as a part of his nature but also as a part of his feelings toward me. I found myself wanting to know him more, to stop the service perhaps and talk with him to understand what made his countenance so rich with feeling. His eyes burned through me, but yet I felt loved and secure. He took the cracker from me with his left hand, and suddenly I noticed a small hammer-like tool in his right hand. The head of it was pointed on both ends like an old-fashioned miner's axe; the handle wooden, firmly in his grasp. He held the cracker to my chest and raised the hammer above his head. I felt only deep awe. I was paralyzed by his eyes. What he was about to do was best for me because it was what he knew I needed, and I found that I trusted him completely. He swung the hammer down through his hand and into me, driving the cracker into my chest. I felt no pain but somehow tasted the cracker in my mouth. The cracker had been filled with a sweet red substance. Jelly is how I remember it now. As I ate it, he pulled the hammer away from my chest and his left hand. I found my hand over my heart where he had hit it, holding a small round glob of the same red substance that filled the cracker. I stared in amazement at it and then looked to him, hoping to ask what it all meant, but he had moved on to the men next to me. I watched him in awe as he continued around the room ministering to each person in a similar way. How could a man be this passionate, this loving? How could a man administer communion in such an effective way? It dawned on me as I sat there. I think this man is Jesus. About that time, He finished and disappeared from the room. I was dumbfounded. What had just happened? Where was I, and had I just encountered Jesus? I moved to another section of the room mingling with people as the service had concluded. I found myself in another square where my brother-in-law and sister sat along with several people from their church. They were cutting up with each other, telling jokes, and laughing together. I wanted to yell at them. Had they not experienced what I had? Had the Jesus man not nailed His hand to their heart and left them with an expression of His blood? Had they not felt His pain? His love? His passion? I awoke.

(From a dream I had at home on April 29, 2021.)

As I recall, there wasn't a lot of value for dreams in my childhood. "You dream what you fear," my Dad would say from time to time, usually after some childhood nightmare or in my teen years, some dream about speaking in public with no pants on.

This made enough sense. I had dreams about ghosts that looked eerily similar to those I had seen in movies. I had others about running from invading Communist or Nazi armies, and still other basic ones of falling. These apparently were fears that lay in my subconscious and were normal enough compared to the dreams that others shared. As a teen entering adolescence, I had sexual dreams, causing me to wake up feeling guilty but also bewildered. "Where did that come from?" I would think.

Though there were dozens of excellent Bible teachers around me in my upbringing and church life, no one seemed to have much to say. "You had a nightmare? You must've watched something scary. Sex dream? Be sure to confess it in prayer and take a cold shower. It's part of puberty, after all."

It wasn't until my mid-30s that I realized these explanations were terribly lacking. This isn't to insult those friends and leaders who gave me the explanations. They were living in the Western world, a culture that had dismissed the power of God's voice in the night. There was a general sense in my home and childhood church that God occasionally spoke outside of His Word, but it was extremely rare and usually only to help with the most significant decisions. To the best of my recollection, I don't remember one story of someone I knew having a significant God encounter in a dream. I knew there were dreams in the Bible, but there were also miracles, resurrections, angel sightings, and God in the flesh, and so I lumped dreams in as a part of the "Bible age," no longer something to expect to happen in my life. After all, I had the Bible to guide me. Why would I need a dream in addition?

At almost 30 years of age, the first crack in my dream ignorance came. In a prayer meeting with a few friends and relatives, we agreed that it was God's will to move from our home in Indiana to West Chester, Ohio, to start a church. We agreed that once we raised $50,000 to fund the startup and moving expenses, we would sell our homes and make the move. With little money committed thus far, we anticipated it would take six to twelve months of fund-raising before we would have close to that number. Before we left that evening, we made a list of individuals to talk to about ideas for raising the funds.

Less than a week later, I met with one of the individuals on that list, along with my friend and fellow church planter Jerod Long. We were in my office at the Bible college where I served as Vice President. The man we talked with was extremely upset that we were leaving the ministry at such a difficult time. He saw Jerod and me as the long-term future of the place and argued with us for two long hours about the decision we were making. At the end of the meeting, he threw his hands up and stunned us. "I had a dream last night," he said. "God told me to take the money I recently made from the sale of my boat and to give it to you. It's $50,000. Who should I make the check out to?"

We were stunned. What a miracle! What an answer to prayer! What a God!

With all that was happening with the move and the launch of the church, I never took the time to consider the ramifications that God had waited until this man fell asleep to *tell him* in a dream to do something that was specific to my need. It seemed to me to be just a miracle and not something that could be developed or sought after again.

Six years into pastoring and newly filled with the Holy Spirit, the call to study what the Scriptures said about dreams came from an unexpected source: My wife Candace.

As I've shared in other parts of this book, Candace has been in step with me at every point of this journey. Most of the steps were shown to me by the Lord, and shortly after, Candace would have an independent experience that confirmed what God was doing in our family and church. This time, though, she was ahead of me.

After hearing the audible voice of Jesus and having some very unique visions, Candace began to study to learn how to steward God's voice and how to continue in dialogue with Him. It wasn't long into the study, reading things like Mark Virkler's *Four Keys to Hearing God's Voice,* that she realized that dreams are a primary way God speaks to us outside His Word.

She began to pray each night, asking the Lord for dreams and keeping a pen and paper by the bedside to jot down all the details from her dreams as soon as she awoke from them while they were fresh on her mind. Soon, my first cup of coffee in the morning was accompanied by her sharing the latest vivid dream that she had experienced and asking for any insight I had in interpreting it. Not being a morning person, I finally laid down some ground rules—well one, actually—no dream-sharing until I've finished that first cup! Frankly, I didn't know what to do with the lengthy dreams she was having or the quotes from Christian writers that she threw at me that insisted that dreams were often messages from God. My pride made me assume that if God hadn't laid this on my heart first, then it was probably a distraction. So, despite her continued consistent dream experiences, I helped her very little with processing or understanding what God was doing in her spirit. Then Jesus showed up in my dream in April of 2021 and hammered a jelly-filled communion cracker into my heart, leaving me undone by His passion and holding on to a measure of His blood. (Now there's a sentence I never thought I'd write in my lifetime!)

The meaning of the dream will be dealt with later, but suffice it to say that Jesus made me take dreams very seriously after that! As I prayed about it, I felt impressed by the Lord to begin to study all of the dreams in Scripture and walk through them in a Sunday morning series at The Father's House. As I put the series together, I read *How to Hear God* by Pete Grieg, and his chapter on dreams put me over the edge. Pete is a pastor in the United Kingdom and the founder of 24-7 Prayer, a movement that has touched the entire earth with prayer rooms and revivals springing up in dozens of nations. His simple treatise on dreams stirred a passion in my heart to hear from God in this manner. I realized that I needed to teach this topic and ask the Lord to forgive me for delaying it so long, even though He had tremendously blessed my wife with a passion and understanding of His night-time voice.

DESIGNED TO DREAM

Did you know that every person dreams an average of five times per night? Years ago, medical researchers seeking to understand more about the science of sleep did a series of sleep deprivation and dream deprivation tests.[57] In the first case, the effects of sleep deprivation were pretty predictable: A decrease in motor skills, a decline in health, and an increase in fatigue. But these researchers went further. They could not only track when a sleeping person began dreaming but also interrupt those dreams without waking the individual. The findings are amazing. Even though these individuals were getting the needed amounts of sleep, the interruption and deprivation

57 New Series, Vol. 131, No. 3415 (Jun. 10, 1960), pp. 1705-1707 (3 pages).
Published By: American Association for the Advancement of Science.

of dreams caused them to have side effects strikingly similar to those deprived of sleep.

God designed us to dream! He made the human body so that its health depends on having continual dreams. We need to dream to stay healthy. Not only this, but once you see what dreams accomplish for individuals in Scripture, you realize dreams improve your spiritual health and relationships.

There are 24 dreams in Scripture[58] ranging from vivid, lengthy, wildly metaphorical dreams to short one-sentence literal dreams of instruction. World leaders like the Pharaoh of Genesis have dreams that, once interpreted, spare the world from the effects of famine. Enemy soldiers preparing for battle against Gideon and his unarmed 300 dream of their demise. Each dream in Scripture is incredible in its own way.

Now, it's easy to read this list and conclude that these dreams were needed because of the importance of the dreamer's mission. Joseph, the man who raised Jesus, had a pretty big task in front of him, and his dreams certainly helped him out several times. And the dreams of the patriarchs: Well, they were the patriarchs, so of course God would speak to them in supernatural ways. I believe this to be a flawed way of interpreting Scripture that leads us away from blessings that God has available to common people like you and me.

Job 33:15–19 (NLT)

15 He speaks in dreams, in visions of the night,

when deep sleep falls on people

as they lie in their beds.

16 He whispers in their ears

and terrifies them with warnings.

---

58 See Appendix 2 for list of Biblical dreams

17 He makes them turn from doing wrong;

he keeps them from pride.

18 He protects them from the grave,

from crossing over the river of death.

God created us to dream! And while we might not need to flee to Egypt any time soon to protect Baby Jesus, we still have responsibilities and needs in front of us that our loving and faithful Father in Heaven longs to assist us with. If He numbers the hairs on our heads, He probably cares about the big business decision that we have ahead of us or the concerns we have about our parenting mistakes. If Jesus is still speaking to us in dreams, logic would tell us to look at some of the things He promises to do in our lives and look for them in our dreams. There are four that stand out to me.

- He cleanses us from sin and its effects.
- He gives wisdom and understanding about our lives.
- He helps us love people more.
- He helps us love our Father more.

I have experienced the fulfillment of these promises in dozens of ways. Verses from the Bible have opened my eyes to my sin or increased my love for the Father. Messages preached, or books written by men and women of God have also had this effect. Dreams are special in that they are often a direct word from the Lord about a topic He wants us to deal with. I've had the effects of sin dealt with due to a dream. Others have caused me to wake up with tears in my eyes in a greater love for my Father in Heaven! Dreams are simply another avenue through which Jesus can communicate to us and fulfill His promises.

Another way to see dreams is to understand they're a bit like a computer reboot, which helps us "defragment" our inner hard drive from the emotional clutter of the day and thus run more efficiently.

> *We have so much going on during the day, so many programs running, that we benefit greatly from a system reboot in the night. Physically, spiritually, mentally, emotionally—dreams recalibrate us in every way. Often it is not just that dreams show us where we are off; they also encourage us that we are doing great and are on the right track...It's important to realize that if we go to bed a little bit "off" or struggling with doubt, God can address that and heal it up for us during the night.*[59]

Of course, there is a significant promise in Scripture that has to do with our dream life. Acts 2 shows us Peter preaching at Pentecost and declaring a new era. The age of the "last days" has come! This age is one that the Prophet Joel saw, and he said that it would be an age that begins with the outpouring of the Spirit and that His arrival would open the eyes of God's family. They would all see visions (see Chapter 10) they would all prophesy (see Chapter 11), and they would all dream.

Acts 2:16–18 (NLT)

16 "No, what you see was predicted long ago by the prophet Joel:

17 'In the last days,' God says,

'I will pour out my Spirit upon all people.

Your sons and daughters will prophesy.

Your young men will see visions,

and your old men will dream dreams.

18 In those days I will pour out my Spirit

even on my servants—men and women alike—

and they will prophesy."

---

59 Virkler, Mark; Virkler Kayembe, Charity. *Hearing God Through Your Dreams: Understanding the Language God Speaks at Night* (p. 101). Destiny Image, Inc.. Kindle Edition.

The Holy Spirit brings dreams with Him! Humanity still dreams without the Holy Spirit, but their dreams shift dramatically when they become filled with His Presence. Here are four ways that the Spirit changes our dream life and speaks to us.

THE HOLY SPIRIT GUIDES US WITH THE DREAMS WE ARE ALREADY HAVING

Even the lost dream. But what solutions do they have for nightmares or anxious visions that cause their hearts to race as they worry about the future? Not many. Sadly, many followers of Jesus remain ignorant to the meaning of their dreams and in some cases, they suffer terribly for it. In 2022, I sat in a Rapha Room with one of our prayer teams, ministering to a 22-year-old girl who had been suffering from violent sexual dreams for over eight years. She goes to a large discipleship-focused, evangelical church. She's been through youth groups, taken missions trips, and interacted with hundreds of Christians and many mature Christian leaders.

No one she met during that time could help her with these dreams. In a two-hour prayer session, the Holy Spirit revealed the root cause of these nightmares, and she was sweetly healed from trauma and set free from the cause of the dreams. I could share a dozen more personal stories like this. One of the great kindnesses that the Holy Spirit does for us is He uses our dreams as insights into what areas of our lives we need Jesus to heal. In this girl's case, two memories were found to be the cause of these terrible nightmares. (She was having several each month.) Though the dreams were bothersome and most likely inflicted by the enemy, they were not the main problem. The Holy Spirit used the dreams to bring the girl to a place where she could find total healing. Over a year later, she has not had one single dream of that nature since. The Holy Spirit takes the dreams that we are naturally having and guides us into the truth about them. This is a part of His function. Jesus told His disciples that, upon His arrival, the Spirit would guide them into all truth. (John 16:13) I believe that most believers have dreams right now that point to a wound in need of the Holy Spirit's guidance and Jesus' healing touch.

THE HOLY SPIRIT SOMETIMES USES DREAMS TO DRAW THE LOST TO JESUS

Several years ago, I received an email with an article from *The Gospel Coalition*. The article detailed accounts of Middle Eastern men and women with Muslim religious backgrounds, converting to become followers of Jesus as a result of dreams.[60] In nearly every case, a Man in white appeared to the dreamer, introduced Himself as Jesus, and detailed to them a way to learn more about Him. Following the instructions in the dream, the dreamers would find a Bible, a pastor, or call a Christian friend, leading to their conversions. In his *Case for Miracles*, Lee Strobel writes:

More Muslims have become Christians in the last couple of decades than in the previous fourteen-hundred years since Muhammad, and it's estimated that a quarter to a third of them experienced a dream or vision of Jesus before their salvation experience. If those statistics are accurate, then this phenomenon of Jesus supernaturally appearing to people is one of the most significant spiritual awakenings in the world today.[61]

The Father's House, where I pastor, financially supports a network of Middle Eastern churches in Iraq, Egypt, and Afghanistan. While having lunch with their founder, I asked him if he had heard of any of the members of these churches having these "man in white" dreams. His response confirmed my thoughts but still surprised me: "About a third of the people who attend our churches had the dream before they ever came."

The ramifications of these accounts are incredible! God is revealing Jesus in dreams to the lost all around the world!

---

60 https://www.thegospelcoalition.org/article/muslims-dream-jesus/ May 31, 2018. Accessed October 11, 2023.

61 Strobel, Lee. *The Case for Miracles* (p. 141). Zondervan,, Kindle Edition.

THE HOLY SPIRIT TEACHES US ABOUT OURSELVES

As I began tracking my dreams and prayerfully attempting to interpret them, I realized that the meaning of most of them was very simple at their core. Don't get me wrong, most of my dreams are filled with all sorts of random details relating to recent conversations, stresses, upcoming events, and relational issues. The contents of my dreams include strange occurrences, wild imagery, and laughable events. But at their core, the meaning usually addresses one thing the Lord wants to reveal about me. Take my hammer-swinging, fiery-eyed Jesus dream that I shared at the beginning of the chapter. Though it has dozens of things that I have gleaned from it, one simple meaning of it is that I need to take communion much more seriously. So in my personal devotions and the culture of the church where I serve, communion is a much bigger deal now than before I had the dream. I've had dreams that told me I was nervous about events that were coming soon. Others told me I felt unprepared or vulnerable. The Lord cares about our feelings, and as our Creator, He knows that if our feelings pile up in an unprocessed place, we will be disconnected from Him. This is why He created dreams as a way for us to see what we are feeling. This helps us know what we need to lay down before Him in prayer and surrender.

If you begin to journal your dreams (and I highly recommend you do), most of your early entries will be under the "inner-healing" category. God is simply showing you something in your life that He wants you to address. To get these simple meanings, you'll definitely need to learn the language of metaphor. Building a sand castle while standing on a kitchen countertop in front of a large group of people while not wearing any pants isn't the easiest thing to interpret if you've never learned to look at each part symbolically. (The dreamer is working on something he doesn't expect to last in a place of preparation while feeling extremely vulnerable and worrying about what everyone thinks.)

> *God counsels us nightly in His desire to break through into our lives with His wisdom, love, creativity, and protection.*
>
> – Mark Virkler[62]

THE HOLY SPIRIT HELPS US PROPHESY THROUGH DREAMS

I'm walking through a church hallway. The building is burning down around me. A friend of mine, a pastor in the Midwest, is walking ahead of me but looking back at me, telling me he isn't the one who started the fire. When we get outside, he confronts me and angrily insists it wasn't him. He is less sad about the burnt building and much more grieved that he might be blamed. (A dream I had in the Fall of 2022.)

The majority of dreams you have include other people. Still, it is essential for you, especially if you're new to tracking your dreams, to assume that this dream is for you and not for the person who happened to appear in it. They may have been in your dream because you saw them recently in person or on social media. They may be there because their name has a special meaning that will help in the interpretation of the dream. They may have a position or outstanding quality that speaks to the meaning of the dream. For example, many people from The Father's House dream about me, but because I am their pastor, they've learned that I represent a messenger of Jesus in the dream and that the dream is not for me or about me as a man or friend.

There are exceptions to this. The dream I share above is one of them. The day after I had this dream, I felt impressed to call my pastor-friend and share it with him. I knew he wasn't a big dreamer or the kind of guy who interprets dreams, so I shared a rough sketch of what I thought it could

---

62 Virkler, Mark; Virkler Kayembe, Charity. *Hearing God Through Your Dreams: Understanding the Language God Speaks at Night* (p. 28). Destiny Image, Inc., Kindle Edition.

mean in the form of a question. I asked, "Have you seen something you built fall apart and been unjustly blamed?"

His response was in the affirmative. He shared that he had felt God's call to go elsewhere after leading a church from barely surviving to thriving. However, within months of leaving, the new pastor contacted him about some money their accountant said was missing. The conversation turned aggressive. The pastor felt sure that my friend had run off with it. To make matters worse, the pastor did away with several of the programs that had helped turn the church around under my friend's leadership. As months passed, the church dwindled in attendance, and the pastor kept calling with increasing threats, asking where the money was. Ultimately, the accountant found that the mortgage company that held the loan on the church's building had made some irregular withdrawals, and all the missing money was found.

Though the situation had been over for many months, my friend was still grieved in his heart. Here's the thing: He buried it so deep in his emotions that he didn't know it was affecting him. So God gave his friend (me) a dream about it to help him process it and be unburdened. I led him through prayer to forgive the accusing pastor and to release all of the pain to Jesus. He wept. Jesus was glorified, and I was amazed at the powerful ways that Jesus still uses dreams in our day.

BUT WHAT ABOUT NEW AGE?

Any time I teach on the topic of dreams to a Christian from a conservative background, their eyebrows raise up and a look of suspicion covers their face. The truth is since psychiatrists like Sigmund Freud and Carl Jung did their dream research, the modern world has been focusing more on dreams and their implications on our waking lives. But like any study that excludes Jesus, the answers are shallow at best or dangerous at worst. Don't let Satan take another gift from the Lord by using a spirit of fear and avoiding dreams. Alternatively, please don't use secular or non-Christian spiritual sources to learn about dreams or interpretations. There are dozens of safe, Biblically sound resources that are available to help you on the journey. Check the Bibliography in the back of this book for a list of a few. Pray with me:

> *Father, I know you made me body, soul, and spirit. I believe your Word, and I know that it says you speak in dreams. I believe You have much to say to me. I surrender my dream life to you. I ask you to search me and know my heart, and I invite you to share your discoveries with me in dreams. I ask you for the gift of Holy Spirit-led dreams that I can remember. I also ask for a spirit of wisdom and discernment in interpreting them. Thank you for being such a loving Father that you care about the contents of my heart. Create in me a pure and soft heart that I might see you and hear you in much clearer ways. In Jesus' mighty name, Amen!*

Dream on, my friends!

CHAPTER 10

SEEING IN THE SPIRIT

> *I pray that the eyes of your heart may be enlightened in order that*
> *you may know the hope to which he has called you, the riches of his*
> *glorious inheritance in his holy people.* (Ephesians 1:18, NIV)

Have you ever had a vision?

In January of 2021, I was sitting at my kitchen table enjoying a cup of coffee and the next three chapters of my daily Bible reading. My Bible reading schedule for that morning had me in Ezekiel chapter one. The Old Testament is filled with amazing encounters and visions from God, but Ezekiel's experiences rival them all.

In chapter 1, Ezekiel experiences the Glory of God in a vision while standing on the bank of a canal in Babylon. Off in the distance he sees a thunderstorm coming toward him. As it gets closer, he realizes that this is no ordinary storm. There is metal swirling in the midst of the storm cloud and a brilliant light reflecting off the metal. As Ezekiel looked closer he saw four beasts. Their appearance is similar to the cherubim that are described in other parts of Scripture. These are the angelic beings assigned as escorts to the glorious Presence of Yahweh. Each cherub has four faces on one head. These four faces are those of a human, a lion, an ox, and an eagle. The covering of their bodies appears as burning stones shifting throughout their bodies. They have four wings. Each creature has a wheel with them. These wheels are their spirits, and wherever the Holy Spirit went, the spirits of the cherubim followed along with their bodies. When they move, their wings sound like the roar of the ocean combined with the thunderous voice of God.

Above this angelic storm cloud, Ezekiel saw a throne. On it sat a being that had the appearance of a man. His upper body appeared as molten metal and his lower body appeared as flames of fire. There was brilliant light all around that appeared as a rainbow. Ezekiel says that he fell down in realization that this was a vision of the glory of God.

I've read this passage dozens of times. It's mysterious and strange. The imagery found in this one chapter points to dozens of other chapters in the Old Testament. But this time as I read it, I felt the Holy Spirit prompt me to take some notes about what Ezekiel saw. The Lord wanted me to understand this vision more clearly.

As I finished outlining the different aspects of the vision, my study was interrupted by my wife. Candace had been praying in our bedroom upstairs when God struck her with a vision. I could tell she was both amazed and bewildered. She sat down next to me, completely unaware of what I had been working on, and shared her vision.

"I saw a thunderstorm come into our room. At first I thought this meant that God was sending a refreshing rain, but as the cloud came closer I could see these beasts inside. They had different faces on them I saw a man, an ox, and a lion. Later, I think I saw a bird like a hawk or eagle. Around them were these wheels, they looked like light blue swirls, spinning around the room, and the beast would follow them."

"Was there a giant white cloud above them?" I asked.

Her head cocked to the side, confused by the question. "How did you know that?" she asked.

Not answering, I went on. "Was there a throne above the cloud, and did you see a man in white?"

Tears filled her eyes. "I thought you were going to think I was crazy as I shared this vision. Have you seen it before?"

I began to slowly read Ezekiel 1 to her. At this point in our marriage, Candace was not a student of the Bible. She was a busy mom, who read the New Testament regularly a chapter per day, was diligent to pray, and passionate about worship, but she was quite unfamiliar with Ezekiel or the other major prophets.

As I read the passage slowly to her, she wept and praised Jesus. Though at that time, we did not fully understand why God had done this, it became unmistakably clear that while I had been studying Ezekiel's 2,500-year-old vision of God's glory, Candace had been experiencing it on the floor of our bedroom.

Skeptics could certainly pick this story apart. Certainly Candace's subconscious has parts of this vision stuck away in some memory cell, put there one fragment at a time over decades of messages and Sunday school lessons. Others might say, she or I are exaggerating or worse, just making it up.

But what if it's true? What if the God who promised visions to His people in the "last days" actually took an overworked pastor's wife and deposited a vision of His Glory in her? I can tell you with absolute certainty that God still gives visions, and that on a January day in 2021, He gave an incredible one to my wife.

WE WERE MADE TO SEE IN THE SPIRIT

Since He finished Creation, the Lord has been speaking to man through the method of visions. We are visual creatures, and it was God who made us this way. This visual side of us is a part of being made in God's image. When God created things, the Word tells us that He would stop and look at it. He analyzed it, studied it, wondered at it, and then enjoyed it, declaring it to be "good." Adam and Eve were made the same way. Adam looked on the animals that God had made and named them. He looked on Eve and Eve back at him and pure romance ensued freed from the guilt and shame that so often distorts sexuality today. It's important to note that their innocence allowed them to see things the way that God saw them. Without sin, they didn't see their nakedness. They could see angels. They could walk and talk with God in Eden's paradise. They could not, however, see their own vulnerable and exposed state. Their peace with God prevented it.

Then the Serpent stepped in. He taught them to see things differently. As they thought of God in a different light, they saw the forbidden fruit with a different perspective. Their distrust of God caused them to now desire the fruit. Once they disobeyed God, their eyes were opened (Genesis 3:7) and they could now see things as being good or evil, and the first evil thing they saw was each other. They were naked sinners who had rebelled against God. So they hid. With eyes that were now aging and dying, Adam and Eve saw two worlds begin to split apart. What was always one line of sight became two. The natural world continued, but immediately started degrading. The spirit world began to disappear. The entrance to Eden was lost. The angels guarding it would fade from view in generations to come. With the reset of a worldwide flood, the ordinary person would no longer see much in the spirit.

There were exceptions. Starting with Abraham, God began to raise up prophets who in many cases were "seers." These were men and women who played a critical role in the unfolding revelation of God's redemptive plan. These prophets experienced visions in the night, glimpses of the spirit world in their mind's eyes, and open visions—spiritual revelations experienced with physical eyes. Abraham saw the fire of God pass through the split carcass of a goat. Jacob wrestled with a man who disappeared at sunrise. Moses saw a burning bush that was not consumed with fire. David experienced several visions and recorded them in the Psalms. My favorite is Psalm 18. David sees fire and smoke proceeding from the mouth of God before He leaves Heaven's temple and rides across the sky on a cherub. Now that's a superhero scene I can't wait to see!

Ezekiel, Daniel, and Isaiah each experienced visions of God's throne room or glory, as did nearly all of the prophets whose names grace Old Testament books. These visions marked them in such ways that they wrote and preached as men on fire. Risking their lives and carrying enormous shame, they carried the Word of the Lord to His people suffering rejection, but remaining determined, driven by memories of encountering the brilliant Glory of their Maker.

In 1 Kings 6, Elisha stood with his terrified servant. The servant could see the vast enemy army. Elisha could see the vast heavenly army. Seeing his servant's fear, Elisha prayed, "O Lord, please open his eyes, that he may see."

So the Lord did, and the servant saw the mountains around the city covered with the angelic army.

These revelations from the Spirit are not limited to the Old Testament. Onlookers at Jesus' baptism saw the Holy Spirit descend in a bodily form like a dove. Believers at Pentecost saw tongues of fire resting on each other's heads. Like his Old Testament prophetic predecessors, Stephen saw Jesus in the throne room. Saul of Tarsus saw Jesus in brilliant light and was blinded and converted, transformed into the Apostle Paul. While waiting on lunch, Peter had a vision where he was commanded to eat unclean animals. The interpretation would lead to the salvation of millions of Gentiles. The Lord saved the most intense spiritual vision for last. Revelation, the entire final book of the Bible, is a series of intense visions, revelations of King Jesus and the "Heaven and Earth" world He will one day completely rule.

If you're a follower of Jesus, then I know you would completely agree with me that God loved to speak through visions in Scripture. Where you might have some concern, though, would be in relation to visions that supposedly come from God today. It's not only Christianity and Judaism that have visions in their traditions. Buddhists, Hindus, and Muslims each have visions as some part of their religion.

Alleged Christians have used visions to depart from the orthodox tenets of Biblical Christianity. History is filled with such claims—deceivers lying about visions to manipulate the naive, or deceived individuals following visions straight out of the true faith. The most well-known example is Joseph Smith's angelic visitations and the eventual formation of the Church of Latter-Day Saints. All this has led to a significant level of skeptical resistance to any mention of visions in the Kingdom of God.

So with all the deception that exists, is there any room left for seeing in the Spirit? Again, we turn to the Scriptures for the answer. At the formation of the church at Pentecost, Peter explained the phenomena of wind, fire, and tongues to onlookers by quoting from Joel.

This is what was uttered through the prophet Joel: And in the last days it shall be, God declares, that I will pour out my Spirit on all flesh, and your sons and your daughters shall prophesy, and your young men shall see visions, and your old men shall dream dreams. (Acts 2:16-17)

Peter's words tell us that Pentecost began the age in which all Christians would dream, prophesy, and have visions. Paul chimed in on this, too, in his letter to the Church at Ephesus written 30 years after Pentecost.

I pray that the eyes of your heart may be enlightened in order that you may know the hope to which he has called you, the riches of his glorious inheritance in his holy people. (Ephesians 1:18, NIV)

Paul is praying for a church that is already filled with the Holy Spirit to have the eyes of their heart opened. His prayer looks strikingly similar to that of Elisha some 700 years earlier; "Lord, open their eyes." Despite the deception, manipulation, and naivety that surrounds the topic of visions, the Holy Spirit is calling believers to see with eyes of faith. What Satan took from man in the Garden, God is returning to His Church.

THE POWER OF IMAGINATION

As we saw in the chapter on Inner Healing, God has given us the gift of imagination. Little children tend to see more in the Spirit because they have stronger imaginations. No wonder Jesus calls us to have childlike faith. I remember one morning while Candace and I were reading our Bibles that our daughter Claire came down from her bedroom. She was about four years of age at the time. As she passed by us on the way to the kitchen, paused, raised her eyebrows, and said, "Mommy, your Bible is on fire!" Then, without another word, she walked on to get started on her breakfast.

One issue is that many of us think of the imagination as a place to formulate fantasy. We think of the "fibs" that children tell and assume that imagination is a whimsical place of deception. But just as our minds can be instruments of righteousness or sinfulness, our imaginations can be given to the Lord as a place of fellowship with Him. The Bible is filled with imagery. Have you ever taken time to picture it in your mind's eye? In Revelation, Jesus is described as a man on fire. His hair is white as snow, and his feet like molten bronze. His eyes are filled with fire, and His face shines with the brilliance of the sun. This is an incredible picture! John gives us this because he wants us to imagine it. Sadly, most people would rather turn to artificial intelligence to generate some image of it. We've allowed technology and culture to take away one of our main sources of seeing in the Spirit.

So let's try a simple exercise.

In a moment, I want you to close your eyes and imagine a cross. Ask the Holy Spirit to help you. Take a few seconds once you've imagined it to notice the details. Okay, now do it.

What did you see? I've asked dozens of people over the years to imagine a cross without any other explanation, and I'm always amazed by the answers I get. Here are the five most common responses.

- Some saw Jesus on the cross.

- Some saw a brown cross with a purple robe on it.

- Some saw a cross in a Garden with flowers around it.

- Some saw a black cross in a dark room.

- Some saw a wooden cross surrounded by light.

- Though it's not the most common, some try to imagine as hard as they can, and see nothing.

The reason I do this exercise with people is to help them begin to discern the matters in their hearts that keep them from experiencing visions from the Lord. For instance, if you saw Jesus hanging on the cross in your imagination, it could mean several things. It could mean that you have a Catholic background and always saw crosses with Jesus on them. It could mean you have a "martyr-spirit," and that as Jesus continues to suffer (in your imagination), you must perpetually suffer in order to please the Lord. It could mean that you are stuck in your faith and have not been able to visit the empty tomb and see that Jesus has conquered everything that you are facing. Our imaginations tell us a lot.

Of course, becoming a seer involves more than just our imaginations. There is a sovereign work of God where He reveals things to us that we simply could never have imagined. He gives us visions in our hearts and on rare occasions, he thins the veil between the natural world and the spirit world, allowing our physical eyes to witness spiritual realities. We call these "open visions."

DEVELOPING THE GIFT OF SEEING

Beyond simply asking the Lord for the gift (which we will do at the end of this chapter), there are five factors to consider as you prayerfully seek God's help in recovering the ability to see in the Spirit. They are your past, your purity, your pliability, your practices, and your persistence.

CONSIDER YOUR PAST

One of my favorite movies around Christmas is the corny classic *The Santa Clause.* In it there is a scene where skeptical stepdad Neil is talking to his wife, Laura, about when he stopped believing in Santa. Laura has told him of a time nearing adolescence when she desperately wanted a "Mystery Date Game," but lost her faith in Santa when the game never appeared under the tree. Neil, the extreme cynic, in an unlikely moment of vulnerability, admits, "I was three, and I wanted an Oscar Meyer weenie whistle. Christmas came, and no weenie whistle…"

"You were three!" Laura responds in shock, having a hard time believing that someone so young could lose their Christmas spirit.

As we consider our past, it's important for us to look back on a time when we turned off our imaginations. Most of us are like Laura. Around adolescence, an awakening occurred where the biology of our bodies and the influence of people around us caused us to lose that childlike faith. For others, something extreme or traumatic can happen, causing a premature severance to our childishness. Regardless of when your imagination stopped becoming a valuable tool, it is helpful to go back to those events and surrender them to the Lord.

CONSIDER YOUR PURITY

As you are working through your past, you may discover some events that destroyed any spiritual imagination that you had. One of the many repercussions of pornography and toxic forms of visual entertainment is that it rewires our brains,[63] forming new channels in our minds, chemically enhancing our lust while simultaneously scorching our ability to see in the Spirit. Satan's answer to a beautiful vision of God's glory that transforms for a life of good, is an image bomb of perversion that bludgeons the

---

63 See *Wired for Intimacy,* William Struthers, Intervarsity Press, 2009.

imagination and conscience and distorts love and intimacy for a lifetime of anger and dissatisfaction.

Consider these words from our Lord. *"Blessed are the pure in heart for they shall see God."* It's not complicated. A pure, undefiled conscience washed in the blood of the Lamb and sprinkled clean with the daily water of the Word, will experience God's presence in a visual way. God is love, and those who are pure can experience and receive His love without shame or fear. A perverse and distorted heart, however, cannot receive His love because the voices of accusation and the images of lust and degradation combine to turn the soul away from the Lord.

If I had read the previous two paragraphs seven years ago, I would have given up on visions. My struggles with lust and forays into pornography had covered me in shame. But God healed me. Since then, I can join in with John Newton, the Apostle Paul, and so many others singing, "Once I was blind, but now I see."

While visions are not a daily occurrence, it is rare for a month to go by without my having some tangible, God-glorifying vision that leaves me in a puddle of tears overwhelmed by the kindness of God. Once you are free from the grip of perversion, take great care to protect your eyes from the perverse side of Hollywood, social media, and the seductiveness of our culture. In our ministry, we've learned to pray for "sanctified imaginations."

CONSIDER YOUR PLIABILITY

The Holy Spirit says, "Today, if you hear His voice, do not harden your hearts…" (Hebrews 3:7-8)

Another reason people struggle with the visual side of the Christian life is their trust in our Heavenly Father has been affected. Just as the Serpent changed Eve's perspective towards God in the Garden, it is easy for us to have a perspective towards God that blinds our hearts. Seeing in the Spirit is a gift from the Father that we cannot receive and use until we trust that He loves us and will care for us. If we have been raised in unsafe religious environments where performance and asceticism were emphasized, we will struggle to trust our Father's kindness enough to let Him show us things. Instead, we will feel towards him the same way we might feel towards a fright-inducing horror film. Our eyes will be partially opened, but we will dread the scary revelation that could pop out at any time. In this case, our hearts have scabs that need treatment and healing, and as they fall off, so too will the scales that cover our spirit-eyes.

The prophet Ezekiel also warned of another kind of hard heart, the heart of stone. If we are rebellious in any way towards the Lord we will not see the things that He desires to show us. Instead, we are ripe for revelations of deception and destruction. False prophets with false dreams and destructive visions abound. Paul warns in Galatians of Satan's ability to appear even as an angel of light deceiving people with heresy while appearing as a true messenger. People who are in rebellion are unwilling to admit that the visions they have received go against the clear teaching of God's Word, and therefore keep a hold on their vision while it drags them beneath the surface of Satan's influence, often causing collateral damage with it.

We remain pliable by participating in a community of Jesus-loving people, submitting our spiritual experiences to them for their input and discernment, serving them with love as unto Christ, and worshipping Jesus alongside of them.

We remain pliable through humble devotion and service to King Jesus. His will be done, not ours. If we are submitted to Him, we will enjoy the fruit of many revelations from His Word and through His Holy Spirit.

CONSIDER YOUR PRACTICE

If you want to see in the Spirit, here are some "best practices."

Have a daily routine of prayerfully seeking God's Presence. As we draw near to Him, He will draw near to us.

Develop an ever-open ear that listens for the questions that we are to ask. The Holy Spirit will often suggest questions that we should ask Him. As we ask the right questions, we will receive revelations from the Lord. These revelations will never contradict Scripture. One question that Candace and I have trained our kids on is, "Where is Jesus?" In every environment that you are in, it should be appropriate to close your eyes, take a deep breath, picture the room in your imagination, and ask, "Jesus, where are you? What are you doing right now? Is there anything you want me to do?" The answers to these questions are often amazing. Jesus loves to show us what He is doing, and He often uses our imagination to communicate it.

Form a Biblical imagination. Next time you are working through a passage of Scripture, take what you have read, close your eyes, and ask the Holy Spirit to help you imagine it. You might be amazed at what He shows you from His Word when you take the time to meditate on it with your sanctified imagination.

> *Father,*
>
> *In the mighty name of Jesus, open the eyes of my heart that I might see more of what You are doing in my life. As Jesus only did what He saw you doing, help me to follow His example. Show me mysteries from your heart that, once unveiled, will help people experience your love and presence in greater ways.*
>
> *Amen*

CHAPTER 11

THE GIFT WE ALL SHOULD WANT

> *Learning to hear God's voice—his word and his whisper—is the single most important thing you will ever learn to do. I'm not exaggerating. Hearing God is not peripheral; it is integral to human history. Neither is it an optional extra for wild-eyed mystics and those who happen to be spiritually inclined. Hearing God is essential to the very purpose for which you and I were made. Without it everything falls apart. But when we learn to love God's Word—to listen and obey—everything aligns.*
>
> – Peter Greig[64]
>
> *I wish you all would prophesy.*
>
> – Apostle Paul

---

64 Greig, Pete. *How to Hear God: A Simple Guide for Normal People* (p. 3). Zondervan, Kindle Edition.

Isn't it funny how you can read a passage dozens of times and still miss the point? I think this is what has happened to me and many others in the Body of Christ with 1 Corinthians 14. Evangelicals trying to avoid controversy but dedicated to preaching through each passage of Scripture will preach on "order in the church." Pentecostals might take a different approach, using it as a launching pad for a message on the need for more tongues in the church. In my Baptist upbringing, the chapter was just skipped altogether.

As I began this foray into a greater understanding of the Gifts of the Holy Spirit, I was surprised to discover that though I had seen the word "prophecy" dozens of times in reading through the New Testament, I didn't actually know what it meant. I was an elementary student when the Left Behind series took the Christian fiction world by storm. The topic of prophecy came to mean, in my mind, a discussion about the return of the Lord.

As I went further into education, prophecy seemed to be about images of charts, endless debates about timing, and extensive explanations of dispensations and predictions. Prophecy seemed to be a bunch of speculation, an attempt to tie together a bunch of loose ends to create an understanding of Christ's return that was clear as mud. Thankfully, the gift of prophecy has nothing to do with this.

Imagine with me that you have the privilege of hosting the Apostle Paul for a weekend. He visits your home, attends church with you, and lets you buy him lunch afterwards. As you eat your meal together, you lean in and ask him for any advice on how to walk closer to Jesus. I believe it wouldn't be too long before you began to discuss the gift of prophecy.

WHAT IS PROPHECY?

Author and Pastor Sam Storms defines prophecy as "the human report of a divine revelation…the speaking forth in merely human words of something God has spontaneously brought to mind."[65] Prophecy involves sharing with a person what you've heard from God. The Gift of prophecy is vital because it involves hearing God with purpose. It is an opportunity for us to tune in to His voice so that we may bless His children. As I write this chapter, my son Clarke's 11th birthday is approaching. A teacher in our church just called me and asked for ideas for getting Clarke a birthday gift. I was pleased to talk to him about the best ways to love my son.

Prophecy is a great way to feel God's favor on you, because you are asking Him for help in loving on His kids. One thing I've learned in teaching on the subject of prayer for 20 years is that a life of prayer involves asking great questions. The Lord loves it when we ask Him how to bless others. A simple but great prayer to add to your daily routine is simply, "Lord, is there something you want me to say to _____?" (For a list of great questions to ask in prophecy, see the "Revelation 2 & 3 Prophecy Model" in Appendix 3.)

PROPHECY IN THE OLD TESTAMENT

Certainly, not all prophecy feels loving. The Old Testament prophets dropped some hard truths on their listeners. A survey of Books like Ezekiel and Jeremiah will leave you with the impression that prophecy is a burden on the prophet and a heavy judgment for the recipients. Places like Moab, Babylon, and Egypt receive prophetic words of impending doom, while the worst seems to be reserved for Israel. Old Testament prophets were watchmen who stood before the Lord and saw the dangers that were coming. They called for repentance, pointing out the evils of their culture.

65Storms, Sam. *The Beginner's Guide to Spiritual Gifts*, p. 110. Baker Publishing Group, Kindle Edition.

Prophetic warnings were in the covenant that God made with the Israelites at Mount Sinai. In his final words to his people, Moses wrote, "If you do not obey the voice of the Lord your God or be careful to do all his commandments and his statutes that I command you, …the Lord will send curses, confusion, and frustration in all that you undertake and do until you are destroyed and perish quickly…" (Deuteronomy 28:15, 20)

Prophets confronted kings about their sins, called out cultures for their idolatry, and brought natural disasters upon their nations through simple declarations. If this is our only understanding of prophecy, we will either shy away from it or misuse it for the hurt of anyone to whom we might speak.

Not all Old Testament prophecies are condemning. Consider the hope that Isaiah gives in various messages: "A virgin shall conceive…they shall call His name Immanuel…He will save His people from their sins." Or the many prophecies of the Second Coming of Christ when the lion will lay down with the lamb and the Prince of Peace will become King over all.

Prophecy is reporting what God is saying, and in the era of the Comforter, the Blood, the Great High Priest, and the Spirit of Adoption, God is saying some beautiful things.

PROPHECY IN THE NEW TESTAMENT CHURCH

Just as the Cross of Christ satisfied the wrath of God towards His people, it also created an opportunity for greater access to God. It has always been in God's heart that all of His people should know and speak His Word. As far back as Moses, we see the cry that all of God's people would prophesy.[66] Without the Cross and ministry of the Holy Spirit, this was impossible, but as we've seen with dreams and visions when the Spirit was poured out on Pentecost, hearing and sharing the voice of God became available to all people.

---

66 See Numbers 11:29.

Twenty years after Pentecost, as Paul traveled throughout Asia Minor planting churches, it is apparent that he built them with a culture of prophecy. In his first letter to the Church at Corinth, he corrected the ways that they operated in the gifts, emphasizing the importance of prophetic ministry as a means for building each other up. This means that he had already instilled a culture of gifts in his time planting the church. After his departure, the Corinthian church had gone off the rails. Division, perversion, disorder, and pride all threatened to destroy their assembly, yet in all of the chaos, Paul encouraged *more* prophecy, imploring them to all focus on it.

In his letters to other churches and leaders, the theme continues. Paul tells the Church at Thessalonica to not despise prophecies and to the Romans, he includes prophecy in a seemingly less supernatural list of spiritual gifts. He reminds Timothy, a pastor in Ephesus, of prophecies received. In Acts, Paul receives prophecy from men like Agabus. If you approach this topic without bias, it is clear that prophetic ministry was a major part of New Testament church ministry.

Whereas many church environments today involve one man speaking and a team of people leading in singing, the early church involved less stage time and more voices. They gathered in houses and in town squares, and apparently, each person had something they had received from the Lord that they were given the opportunity to share.

> *Each of you comes together with a hymn, a lesson, a revelation, a tongue, or an interpretation…let two or three prophets speak and let others weigh what is said…you can all prophesy one by one so that all may learn and be encouraged.* (I Corinthians 14:26-31)

Imagine a church where everyone came prepared to bless and encourage another person! The cancer of celebrity Christianity would die, and the nutrition of God's Word spreading through a praying church would blossom.

In 2020, fresh off months of quarantine due to the COVID-19 pandemic, Jerod Long and I challenged each other to instill this culture into The Father's House. We began assembling in midweek small groups and watching some YouTube videos of simple teaching on hearing God's voice and learning to walk in the supernatural spiritual gifts. After several weeks of discussion and teaching, we began to take time with the groups to listen to the Lord and share what they heard. Once they grew comfortable with this, we began to take turns as a group praying and listening for one couple at a time. These prayer times were incredible. Everyone in the groups took it very seriously, and we found ourselves hearing God speak and responding with worship late in the night. During that year, my children had a record number of tardies at school because our prayer meetings were going until past one a.m., two or more nights per week.

The Apostle Paul said that when prophecy is shared correctly, the "secrets of the listener's heart are disclosed, and so, falling on his face, he will worship God and declare that God is really among you."

This began to be a regular experience. People would receive from their church family what God had told them during their time of prayer and break down in tears, sharing deep wounds and dreams hidden in their hearts and experiencing healing in a depth that they never thought possible.

One night, it was Candace's and my turn to receive. We sat on a ratty old couch that we kept in our church basement, and five couples from one of our groups surrounded us, laid hands on our shoulders, and began to pray. They interceded for us to the Lord for about fifteen minutes, and by the time they were finished, nearly all of them were crying. I could feel a holy presence in the room. The Good Shepherd was with us, and He was leading this now.

It had been a particularly hectic day for my wife and me. Our son has a medication that is very important for his treatment, and our pharmacist had rudely told us that he could not continue filling the prescription. My wife had lost it right there in the grocery store. Normally soft-spoken and meek, she let the pharmacist know that his oversight would cause pain to our son and that his carelessness in not communicating with us was unacceptable. I was surprised by her anger but proud of her for defending our kids. She made her point. The pharmacist was wrong. Four years later, they are still filling that prescription every month.

As we sat on the couch that night, feeling the comforting holy weight of God in the room, one of our men, Justin, began to share what he felt God had given him on our behalf. "Candace," he said, "I believe the Lord showed me you as a lioness. You were up on two hind legs roaring in defense of your family, specifically your cubs. Jesus wants you to know He loves the way you love your kids."

We had told no one of our run-in at the pharmacy. Frankly, we were a little embarrassed at how angry we had gotten with the technician. But here was a rookie prophetic voice, one of our dearest brothers in Christ, telling us that Jesus had seen the whole thing and that He was okay with it. More than that, He was proud of Candace for what she had done. I remember the hair standing on the back of my neck as Justin delivered that word. God was clearly present in the room and in this time of prophecy. The words Justin said were so simple, but God took them and drove them deep in my heart. This simple prophetic word told us that God saw us, was with us, and found joy in us. Is there any message more important for the church to hear today than that?

God was with you today.

He saw you.

He found great joy in what He saw.

This is the message that transformed a skeptical Nathanael into a radically committed follower of Jesus. When Jesus greeted him with an overly familiar greeting, Nathanael asked, "How do you know me?"

Jesus responded, "(Earlier) when you were under the fig tree, I saw you." There isn't much detail given as to what Nathanael was thinking while under that tree, but the fact that Jesus had seen him, had *noticed* him, and was asking if they could do life together did something deep in Nathanael's heart.

I saw you.

I noticed you.

I want to draw closer to you.

True prophecy conveys the heart of God from one believer to another. It is truly a gift from God. We are given this indescribable privilege to steward the loving heart of God and to deliver it to a person who is in desperate need of it. No wonder Moses and Paul echoed the Holy Spirit in saying, "I wish all would prophesy!" Every believer I know is truly hungry to hear afresh how God feels about them and what He is noticing or desiring to point out in their lives. But of course, because of the sin that exists in our world, this precious gift can be misused. Let's look at some critical guidelines for how to prophesy and how NOT to prophesy.

THE IMPORTANCE OF HEARING CORRECTLY

If you haven't figured it out yet, let me just repeat it again. Life with the Holy Spirit is a call to listen. Seven times to seven churches, Jesus presents Himself as watching each church, seeing their suffering, but not dismissing their struggles, or worse, their sins. He instructs them, encourages them, and in some cases warns them. Each prophetic word delivered by Jesus through the Apostle John is accompanied with this command: "He who has an ear, let him hear what the Spirit says to the churches." (Revelation 2-3)

The last words that Jesus gives His churches is to listen to the Spirit! God is speaking, and because He is a loving God who longs for His people to love each other as much as they love Him, He speaks to us about each other. Once again, as soon as we see what God is doing, we must be aware of how the enemy is counterfeiting. God calls us to share loving, holy, and encouraging prophetic words that build up the believer and glorify God. Satan imitates by bringing gossip and accusation to us, which causes us to judge and condemn. If you don't believe me, take a look at the interactions between Christians on social media. There doesn't seem to be much unity or compassion. One reason for the disdain for local church prophetic ministry is because people with toxins in their hearts, under the guise of prophecy, use their words to gossip about or criticize people, or worse, manipulate people into making poor decisions. Horror stories abound in charismatic circles of people marrying the wrong person because they got some prophetic word that made them feel certain it was God's will.

If our hearts aren't healthy, we shouldn't be prophesying. It's too easy with heart wounds to tune into the wrong voice or, even if we heard the correct thing from God, to add a little bit of our words to His Words as we deliver the message. So before you develop a habit of being prophetic, develop a discipline of listening to God, writing down what you think He said, and only sharing it with one trusted fellow believer. As you take time to do this, you will see in your journaling a cleansing of your heart and an increase in clarity as to what God actually said and what your emotions or even the enemy also said.

One reason that our little ratty couch church basement experiment worked so well at The Father's House was that we had two relatively experienced coaches on hand helping people filter out what they were hearing and giving them a safe space to learn to tune into the frequency of God's voice and to deliver it without any seasoning of their opinions or judgments. With this in mind, I highly recommend walking through this with a small group or online community before you begin sharing words with other people in your church.[67]

---

67 Jerod Long hosts a regular online prophetic training seminar. For more information, visit *fathershouse.tv/prophecy*.

THE IMPORTANCE OF SHARING CORRECTLY

Sometimes, God shows us something about another believer, not as an answer to prayer but as a direction for prayer. There are many people whom God has called to intercession, but who are oblivious. Instead, they keep forcing the prophetic and leave trails of offended people in their wake. The ability to discern what is happening in a person's life can be useful in deliverance ministry, prophecy, and intercession. It is imperative that before you share what you've discerned, you submit to the Lord for His purposes in why He let you see that situation in the first place. For this reason, we have some simple "house rules" wherever I lead ministry when it comes to prophetic words.

- If it's positive or encouraging, share it.
- If it's potentially negative, pray about it.
- If it's negative but dangerous or a warning, speak to a pastor about it before telling anyone else.

These three simple principles can spare you a lot of conflict and can also help your prayer life bear a lot of fruit.

If you share a positive prophetic word, you bear the fruit that comes with building up a believer in his or her holy faith.

If you hold a negative word and begin to pray about it in private, you bear the fruit of bearing another believer's burden and the eventual reward that comes with seeking God in the secret place.

If you take a word of warning to a pastor, you allow him to evaluate the word, and you bear the fruit of humility. If he takes the warning seriously and gives it to the deliverance or counseling team, you bear the fruit of once again having helped someone, even though they may never know it was you who first heard it from the Lord. Let me say that you don't need credit in order to be an effective prophetic voice. Too many people are always inserting themselves into prophetic ministries with "I told you so's." Their boast is their only reward.

YOU'RE PROBABLY NOT A PROPHET

As you begin to step out in boldness and share what you heard from the Lord, do so with humility and meekness. Give people the opportunity to listen and evaluate the word without the pressure of hearing, "Thus saith the Lord!"

In the Scriptures, there are a number of men and women who are given the green light to declare emphatically that what they have heard is from God. Thousands of years later, we call them prophets and prophetesses. But giving an accurate prophetic word does not make a person a prophet. Prophets hold an office and carry a responsibility to God that goes beyond the spiritual gift of prophecy. I have had plumbing repairs and projects that have been my responsibility as the man of the house. I have done those to the best of my ability. But I am not a plumber. I'm not licensed. I don't have a business, and I don't know much about it. Effectively cleaning out a clogged drain doesn't mean I should be printing business cards with "plumber" as one of my job titles. There is a prophetic madness that has been exposed since the 2020 Presidential election, where people who claimed to be prophets made claims in the name of Jesus that are simply not from God. The vast majority of these individuals had taken the local church gift of prophecy and tried to make it into a national prophetic office. They need to turn off their YouTube prediction shows and go back into the small groups of their local churches, encouraging, serving, and loving their brothers and sisters in Christ.

> *If one should be trusted by God to prophesy at the same level as Elisha or Nathan, can one say "Thus says the Lord"? I answer: Why do it? I would say that if you are an Elijah and Elisha and Gad and Nathan rolled into one, follow Jesus' own interpretation of the third commandment in the Sermon on the Mount to refuse to invoke the name of the Lord. It is not necessary to bring anything or anyone greater to validate an authentic word from God. The greatest freedom is having nothing to prove. If you truly have a word from God, it will not return void but will accomplish what God intends (Isa. 55:11).[68]*
>
> – R.T. Kendall

In delivering prophetic words, consider safe and humble approaches. Here are a few examples:

- "I think the Lord gave me something to share with you, but I could be wrong."

- "This is what I think I heard the Lord say to me on your behalf. Does that resonate with you? If not, it may be for someone else."

- "Here is what I think the Lord said. Take some time to pray about it, and let me know if it was truly Him or not. I'll follow up with you later and hope you'll tell me if what I said was helpful or not."

When you admit that you're not infallible in your prophetic gifting, it allows the person to receive it with grace and evaluate it for whatever truth it may contain. Truthfully, most people who are developing in the prophetic hear accurately from the Lord, but struggle to share it without a little of their personality coming through as "hamburger helper." Give them the meat and let them evaluate how to use it.

---

68 Kendall, R.T. *Prophetic Integrity: Aligning Our Words with God's Word*, p. 109. Thomas Nelson, Kindle Edition.

YOU DON'T WANT TO BE A PROPHET

Prophets in the Scriptures were men and women who heard the Word of the Lord under duress. Many were starving alongside their fellow countrymen as they spoke their messages. They were rejected, misunderstood, criticized, imprisoned, and executed. The only thing more painful than being a prophet was being an apostle. People who claim to be prophets today either do so with the scars of suffering that validate that they have been marked under the presence of God, or they are celebrity prophetic peddlers who tickle ears for money. The Word of the Lord spoken to a prophet in the secret place is the burden of the Lord. It often makes their bones burn, their stomachs nauseous, and their emotions sorrowful.

If an American today claims to be a national prophet, watch for his tears. Our nation is in trouble, and anyone making stock predictions or encouraging entrepreneurism is likely a false prophet. R.T. Kendall wrote, "I hope I'm not being unfair, but many prophets today only give words of encouragement with the aim of making people feel good. I'm sorry, but such prophecies do not mirror the full image of Jesus, especially as revealed in the book of Revelation. The testimony of Jesus, therefore, means that the prophecy is not only true but in accordance with the entire Word of God… Prophecy will mirror the person and truth of Jesus."[69]

WE NEED PROPHETS

I believe that God will call some people who read this book to become His prophets. I have seen Him call one or two individuals in the churches that I've led. His call is clear to everyone who knows them, as is the burden they carry. Though the call comes with persecution, it also comes with the unspeakable privilege of standing before the Lord and listening to His secrets. These men and women don't call themselves prophets or

---

69 Kendall, R.T. *Prophetic Integrity: Aligning Our Words with God's Word,* p. 101. Thomas Nelson, Kindle Edition.

hold their office over other people. Rather, they spend hours each morning and night listening to God on behalf of others for what He wants to say. God speaks to them in visions, dreams, impressions, conversations, arts, entertainment, and nature, and He holds them accountable to steward everything He tells them. Don't try to be a prophet. It's not something you try. You follow Jesus, and if He wants you to be a prophet, He'll purify your lips with fire, form your heart through humiliation, train your eyes with His Word, mark your life with a burden, and make you a desperate addict to the Scriptures. In doing these things, He will keep you from being too exalted as you deliver the Word of the Lord to your generation.

> *The ability to speak with clarity under persecution requires a high level of prophetic authority and power.*[70]
>
> – R.T. Kendall

WE NEED LOCAL CHURCH PROPHETIC MINISTRY

If my descriptions of being a prophet have made you want to run from this chapter early, I want to encourage you that God wants you to prophesy, and He probably won't make you a weeping prophet in order to do so. Local church prophecy needs to be restored as a routine part of church culture. The voice of God needs to be returned to the church! God is speaking into every situation of life. Where are the men and women who will dedicate themselves to listening on behalf of their local assemblies? Sadly, a misunderstanding of this gift has caused leaders to ban it from their congregations, leaving the seers and hearers out in the cold, bitter at the institutionalized church. Courage, humility, and persistence are needed. "Father,

---

70 Kendall, R.T. *Prophetic Integrity: Aligning Our Words with God's Word,* p. 101. Thomas Nelson, Kindle Edition.

give us a million small groups in a hundred-thousand churches that will learn to be encouraging voices that steward your heart for this generation!"

WE NEED PROPHETIC EVANGELISM

One of the misunderstood benefits of prophetic ministry in a local church is in regards to seeing people become born-again followers of Jesus. Paul seems to indicate in I Corinthians 14 that the gift of prophecy is largely *for* the lost. As we have trained the people in this gift of prophecy, we have prayed that it would not become a tool used for people to just pat each other on the back in some feel-good, supernaturally spiritual way. We want to reach the lost, and we need the power of God to do it. My friend and prophetic voice, Jerod Long, shares this story:

On November 15, 2018, I woke up with the word "apoplexy" plastered on my mind. I had been reading lots of books about prophecy and words of knowledge in that season of my life, so when this strange word appeared I had a hunch that it might be God. I quickly opened the notes app on my iPhone and typed out these words: "Pray for / lay hands on someone who is apoplectic or has apoplexy." I've never used this word in my life.

After I documented the word, I looked up the meaning. I learned that apoplexy refers to a state of incapacitation due to a stroke or brain hemorrhaging. At that time I was an in-home salesman, so all throughout my work day I was on the lookout for some kind of reference to apoplexy.

At the end of the day I went into the office to do some paperwork. When I arrived I saw Jill. Jill was a middle-aged sales associate who was relatively new to the company. She knew that I was a Christian, but up to that point we had not had many spiritual conversations. As soon as I saw Jill, the Holy Spirit whispered to me, "Tell Jill about apoplexy." I took about a minute to plan my approach, and then I asked, "Hey Jill, do you know what spiritual gifts are?" "No," she replied. I said, "Well, in the Christian life, spiritual gifts are ways that the Holy Spirit empowers us so that we can serve and love others well. One of those gifts is called a word of knowledge, and I think that the

Lord gave me a word of knowledge for you this morning. Would you like to hear it?" She said that she was open, so I explained how the word apoplexy was plastered on my mind and I asked if that word meant anything to her. She said, "Yes. My dad, John, was just put into hospice this week because he has apoplexy and he has not recovered. They are expecting him to pass soon if something doesn't change."

As these words were coming out of her mouth, my eyes filled with tears as I realized that this was a bonafide God moment. I took out my phone and showed Jill my notes app. When she read it, her eyes filled with tears too. I said, "Jill, I think the Lord is going to heal your dad. Can we pray together?" She and I went over to the side of the sales room and prayed for John to be healed from his sickness and saved.

One week later, Jill came into work and shared the news that John had miraculously recovered and hospice was sent home. Shortly thereafter, some Christian friends from high school came to visit and they shared the Gospel with him. Jill reported that her dad had "found religion and believed in Jesus." About two years later John died, and I trust that I will see him one day in heaven.

That was my introduction to the ministry of prophecy and words of knowledge. And what an introduction it was! Since that day, I have had the joy of delivering many words of knowledge to many different people in a variety of settings. But Jill and John's story will always hold a special place in my heart. I'm so thankful that I got to play a part in God's rescue plan for John. Praise the Lord!

Are you ready to prophesy? The American church, in particular, is starving for selfless people who, out of a spirit of love, will host the presence of the Lord and listen to what He has to say about those whose paths they will cross.

PRAYER OF ACTIVATION

Father,

In the mighty name of Jesus, I ask that through the Holy Spirit, you would give me the gift of prophecy. Please fill me with a heart of love and help me hear only what You are saying. In your gracious favor, help me to have discernment and wisdom to know when and how I should give words. I believe that you want me to have this gift more than I do so in anticipation, I dedicate myself to be becoming a child of God who listens carefully to the words of his Father.

Thank you for still speaking today. Your compassions never change.

Amen

Don't forget to take some time to look at a powerful tool for learning how to prophesy in Appendix 3.

CHAPTER 12

SPIRIT FORWARD

> *Anyone with ears to hear must listen to the Spirit and understand what he is saying to the churches.* (Revelation 3:22, NLT)
>
> *The Spirit and the bride say, "Come." Let anyone who hears this say, "Come." Let anyone who is thirsty come. Let anyone who desires drink freely from the water of life.* (Revelation 22:17, NLT)

In May 2021, I was lying on my sheepskin prayer rug, praying about a pastor's meeting I had just cancelled. We had made a simple plan to host five pastors at our church for a couple days of discussing the power of the Holy Spirit. Two weeks before it was to begin, three of the pastors had called and cancelled. I had then called the other two to let them know we would not be holding it. I was both disappointed and embarrassed. The Lord has spoken very specifically to me about testifying to pastors about the powerful things He had done in my life and church. It didn't seem very "powerful" or "prophetic" to cancel a meeting. As I expressed my disappointment in prayer, the Lord spoke into my spirit more directly and clearly than I've ever heard before. "Your plan was too small. Don't invite five pastors, invite 50. Rent whatever you need to compensate for your small church facility.

Teach them about all the things I've been doing in your life and church. Call it 'Spirit Forward.'"

I got up from my prayer rug and immediately wrote down the plan for what has become Spirit Forward Ministries. Six months later, in November 2021, we hosted over 60 ministry leaders from 23 churches and testified of what God has done in our lives. These numbers may seem small to you. They are certainly much smaller than the "Pastor's School" Conference numbers that my Grandfather experienced several decades ago. But the fruit of what God has done since that conference has continued to spread.

A pastor from a church in central Indiana left the conference unsure of what he'd just experienced. People had been healed, prophetic words had been given, and prayer and ministry had gone late into the night. Within a year, he opened a dedicated prayer room in the church. Demons began to manifest and people were set free. Soon he and his elders agreed to dedicate their church to hosting the presence of God and listening to His voice. The church has been growing ever since.

A pastor from Central Illinois wrote that he had never been in a room that had such tangible spiritual hunger. He went back to his church and renewed his passion to lead his people in prayer and the love of Christ. His wife was soon baptized in the Spirit. Powerful manifestations of the Holy Spirit began to occur regularly in their church.

A new church was launched in Missouri by one of the men in attendance.

Another pastor in Central Indiana shared that for the first time in his 50+ years on earth, he had experienced the Father's love and had found it in his heart to forgive his earthly father for abandoning him 40 years earlier.

A pastor and staff from Southern Ohio began to teach their church about the voice of God. Prophetic words began to flow and people who had been attending their church for decades began to finally get freedom and live in the abundant life that Jesus has promised.

Another local pastor came for just one night of the conference. After hearing my sermon he walked forward for prayer. After two minutes of prayer he fell under the power of God and the entire room shook. He told me later that God set him free from deep wounds that caused terrible anger in his life. "I've been knocked out twice in my life," he said. "Once in a bar fight before I became a Christian, and the other time was at your church, Ken, under the power of God. God did some heart work on me that I wouldn't have believed if I hadn't experienced it myself."

He dedicated 2023 to his church as being the year of discovering the Holy Spirit.

Another pastor from the South who attended that conference called me several months ago. "Ken, we saw revival break out in our Sunday morning service. People were healed of severe back issues, cancer, and deafness. After seeing these miracles, repentance broke out. People started to come forward and testify of what God was doing in their hearts. How do I keep this going?"

A pastor from Michigan leaned against the wall during the entire prayer time we had. He watched confused and uncertain of what he was seeing. He had questions swirling through his mind. How could all these people pray and receive from the Lord for such lengthy periods of time? And why wasn't he feeling anything in his spirit? Two years later he came to our third Spirit Forward Conference. I preached on having a vision of Jesus. "Go Find Jesus!" I yelled throughout the message. As he closed his eyes, he saw nothing but blackness. It frustrated him. Would God always continue to hide Himself? Finally this pastor broke and came forward for prayer. After being led through a few questions and prayers, he fell on his face and began to weep. He'd had a vision of Jesus and everything was different. A few months later, I spoke with his wife. "It's like he just got saved!" she said. "He's so different. He knows that God loves him in a way that he had never experience before. His church is growing as God sends people to see a man on fire."

I am nothing special. I am not perfect. I am…just a son with a gift. I've been given something to pass on to you. Spirit Forward ministries, this book, and nearly everything I do as a follower of Jesus are in obedience to sharing the gift that the Lord has given me. This is the gift: A testimony that's contagious. Some might call it fire. I'm okay with that. Others might call it faith. I'm not sure I'm spiritual enough for that to be true, but I'll take it. Whatever it is, although I am flawed and have made many mistakes, God has given me something that I am supposed to pass out. It is a call to impartation. It is a call to move forward in the Spirit.

As I look at the darkness that encroaches on the earth, Satan's last gasp before King Jesus returns, I see a desperate need for believers to be refreshed, refilled, or in some cases baptized in the powerful Presence of God's Holy Spirit. They cannot go forward any further in their tradition or human strength. Character and structure will not suffice. They need an unction, a holy touch from Spirit of the Creator that will mark them for the rest of their lives. It is my prayer that this book will serve as a kickstarter for that very thing. I hope as you have read this, that you have gotten hungry, extremely hungry. I urge you not to strive in the flesh or grow discouraged in this hunger. The God who makes us hungry is the God who will feed us to satisfaction. He pours water on the thirsty and satisfies the hungry with the Bread of His Presence. He has New wine for joy, oil for our healing, and fire to light the way that He is leading us in. Ask and receive that your joy may be full!

A couple years back, I was at a pastor's retreat trying to spread some fire. As far as I know, I was the only pastor there who believed in the baptism of the Holy Spirit or the continuation of the supernatural gifts. I tried my best to tell as many stories of miracles that I could without dominating the retreat. Testimonies build faith and lead to outbreaks of God's power, and so I kept plodding along with stories of answered prayers, miraculous conversions, and unexplainable healings. It was hard to keep it up because the theme of the retreat was on having a balanced church! I lead churches to create cultures that are radical for Jesus. Balance is for people who need to walk in their own strength and stay in the boat. Once you start walking on water, balance is a moot point.

Finally, a pastor stopped the retreat and said, "Can we pray for a few minutes? I'm not feeling well, and I've been hearing Ken tell all these stories of healing. Ken, will you pray for me?" Excitement grew in me. Finally the night was getting interesting! I laid hands on him and prayed. Soon his pain diminished, though he was not completely healed. As I turned away, another pastor stopped me and asked me to pray with him. He told me of a teenage girl who was at their teen camp at that moment. She had been one of the more popular girls in their group until a series of debilitating neurological troubles began to occur. They had gotten so bad, she had lost her balance recently and torn the ACL in one of her knees. She was scheduled for surgery a few days later but was still desperate to enjoy some of her senior year in high school and attend this camp. At this retreat, thousands of miles away from this girl and the camp she was attending, the pastors joined together and prayed for her healing.

Later she would call her pastor and tell him the story.

We were worshipping before the evening service when I began to feel heat in my body. Suddenly standing before me was Jesus. He placed His hands on either side of my face and began to speak to me. I fell over immediately. My friends thought I was having another episode, but I pushed them off me. I got up and began to dance, realizing I had been healed. The leaders and counselors at the camp struggled to believe me, but after the doctors looked me over the next day, my surgery was cancelled. I'm healed! Jesus touched me and healed me!

I spoke with the principal who was running the camp that week, and he admitted that though they were singing about Jesus and preaching about Jesus, none of the leaders had a clue as to what to do with a girl who said that Jesus had shown up and healed her body. This was a Baptist camp. Jesus didn't typically do those things in that context.

Upon hearing of her healing, the pastor held a celebration at the church. It sounds like just the kind of thing Jesus would do. Hold a party at church to celebrate a miracle. As the party was going on, the pastor heard God speak to him with a clarity that he'd never experienced before. The Lord directed his eyes to a visitor who had come. It was a man who was slowly moving through the Hall. He had a stick in his hand that indicated that he was blind. "Go pray for him to be healed," the Lord told my pastor friend.

"You're going to heal a blind man tonight?" he responded.

"No, but I will heal him," God said.

Confused but filled with faith, the pastor went to this man and asked if he could pray for his healing.

"For my eyes?" the blind man asked.

Fumbling for words, the pastor said that actually the Lord had told him that He wasn't going to heal his blindness. "I think there is something else He wants to heal, but I have no idea what it is," the pastor said.

So he prayed for healing for the unknown.

Two weeks later he received a letter. This blind man had some questions about Jesus. He'd never been much of a believer until that night two weeks before. No one at the party knew it, but he had been diagnosed with terminal cancer and didn't have long to live. But God had other plans. After receiving prayer from a confused pastor, he went back to the doctors to discover that the cancer was completely gone!

Hallelujah! Testimonies build faith and produce miraculous fruit.

As Jesus prepared His disciples for church life without Him, He spent a great deal of time teaching them about the Holy Spirit. He told them that it was expedient that He go away so that the Spirit could come. When the Spirit came, the disciples began to do the same things that Jesus had done, much to the chagrin of the Pharisees and Temple leaders. Thinking they had gotten rid of this Jesus character, they were now confronted with dozens if not hundreds of people who all were doing what Jesus had been doing. While waiting on Jesus to return, these disciples were moving forward in the power and presence of the Spirit. "Greater works shall ye do!" Jesus had promised, and sure enough, His Words to them came to pass.

That promise still stands today. We have the same Spirit that Jesus had, and we can do the same works, and greater works because Jesus stands at the right hand of the Father in Heaven's throne room interceding on our behalf, ensuring that not one of His promises falls to the ground unfulfilled.

I'm so thankful that in His mercy, He poured His Spirit out on me and that I could be a witness of seeing His promises come to pass. As I close, I want you to extend your hands and receive through the prayer I've written below. It's time for an army of Jesus-loving disciples to move forward in the Spirit of Jesus.

Father,

In the mighty name of Jesus, I ask that you would pour your Spirit out powerfully on each person who picks up or digitally possesses this book. I pray that you would give them what you have given me—the fullness of the Spirit in them from the top of their head to the bottom of their feet. I pray that His mighty power would break off any enemy attachment and heal any ailments in their bodies. I pray that His peace would wash over them and that every bit of fear, anxiety, and depression would leave them never to return. I pray that the fire of the Spirit would blaze in them so brightly that everyone they know would eventually catch ablaze in the love, the kindness, and the favor of your Holy Presence. Give gifts generously to them, Papa. You are the best Gift-giver!

Come, Holy Spirit. For the sake of Jesus, Come. Descend on this reader.

Now unto the Lamb, the Holy King of all kings, be glory, blessing, honor, and power forever and ever.

Amen

APPENDIX 1:
THIS KIND OF MIRACLE

I wrote in chapter 1 of my grandfather's sermons about God's power and miracles. Here is one called, "This Kind." It's transcribed from a sermon preached by Dr. Jack Hyles at a Sword of the Lord Conference in the 1970s.

One Sunday morning, we were having services in the Civic Center, downtown Hammond, while we were enlarging our auditorium. I preached and gave the invitation. A man who had been blind many, many years, with the nerves in his eyes gone, came running down the aisle saying, "Pastor, Pastor! I can see! I can see!"

I was preaching on a Sunday night in Hammond. I stopped in the middle of my sermon and said, "God is going to do a miracle right now." (I have never said that in my life before nor since.) I said, "Tonight something miraculous is going on in this room. I don't know what it is."

I got a letter the next week from a Moody Bible Institute student who was in our services. She said, "I have an eye that I have never seen with. When you said that last Sunday night, I saw through that eye!"

Now, how does one get that? You feel that when you come to know God, when you walk with God, spend time with God, and beg and pray, and sometimes fast.

People often say, "I want to go see what this fellow looks like who pastors one of the largest churches in the world." They come. They say, "Well, is THAT Jack Hyles? There is nothing unusual about him!? No, but he spends a lot of time with Somebody Who is pretty special! This kind, I mean this kind of miracle where folks in town know that God does something down there, comes by nothing but by prayer and fasting.

Years ago in Texas, one of our fine ladies called me on the phone. She was weeping. "Pastor, my little girl is four years old. She has cancer of a kidney and we have to have a kidney removed."

They went to the hospital. The doctors removed the kidney eaten up with cancer.

It was only a few weeks until this same lady called again. She was beside herself. "Pastor, she has cancer in the other kidney and the doctors say there is no hope. Pastor, doesn't the Bible say something about anointing with oil and praying and fasting?"

Singer Bill Harvey went with me to the home on the east side of Garland, Texas. I took a little olive oil. We got down on our faces and prayed and confessed our sins. I said, "Dear Lord, I pray You would heal this little baby." Bill did the same thing. We anointed her on the head with oil. I was in Texas just a few months ago and a beautiful young lady walked up. "Dr. Hyles, do you know me?" "No, I don't." "I'm 22 years of age. Do you know me now?" "I just have one kidney. Do you know me now?" I said, "You are not the little girl we anointed who had the kidney cancer?" "Yes, I am." She said, "I am going to get married in a few weeks. Brother Hyles, I have been well now all these years."

A dad lay in the hospital dead. His death certificate had been made out. The funeral service was announced in the church service. He had been dead for hours. A deaf young man walked inside that room and he had something he wanted to say to his daddy before his daddy died. He pulled the sheet back off his daddy's dead body and said, "Daddy! Daddy! Daddy!" Those dead eyes opened, that dead mouth spoke, and that dead body lived for another day so that boy could tell his dad some things he wanted to tell him. The man died. The boy had some more he wanted to tell his daddy. The fellow had been dead for a while. The son walked back in and talked to his daddy who had been declared dead twice and whose service had been announced in church again to be the next day. The night before the service was conducted, that man who had been lying dead for hours and hours with a sheet pulled over his head—that son, who is a deaf lad about 22 or 23 years old, said, "Daddy! Daddy! Daddy!"

And the Lord in Heaven seemed to say, "Make up your mind when you are through talking to your dad." The Lord said to the dad, "Go back down there for a while; John wants to talk to you." And his eyes opened and his voice spoke and his lips moved, and God proved again He can do anything but fail." "This kind can come forth by nothing, but by prayer and fasting."

We had a lady in our church with a tumor on her brain. The doctor had shown me the X – ray several days before. I went to the hospital the morning she was to have surgery. (The doctor said it would be a five – to seven-hour surgery.)

I took a bottle of olive oil. I put a little on her forehead and prayed, "O God, heal this lady and show that doctor there is a God in Heaven Who still perform miracles." They rolled her up to surgery. I was waiting out in the hall. In less than an hour they rolled her back. The doctor was beside her. I said, "Doctor, is surgery over?" "She didn't have surgery." "Why?" "The tumor is gone!" You don't get this because you have a D.D. You don't get this because you have been to college and seminary. You don't get this because you have taken Strong's theology. You get this because you realize there is nothing in the world you can do, and you throw yourself at the mercy of God Almighty and say, "O my God, You have to do something!"

Two weeks ago I was in a certain city. Folks brought a little three-year-old child to me. They said, "Dr. Hyles, the doctor said both of us were sterile and could not have a baby, and a few years ago out East you took a little bottle of olive oil and anointed my wife's head and mine. You prayed for God to open her womb and give life to my seed. Brother Hyles, within a year's time we had a baby and we want to show you the baby."

What we need in our Baptist churches are some preachers who know God, walk with God, and can say, "I spend time in prayer, I fast, I beg and plead. Night after night I walk with God and day after day I walk with God."

"This kind can come forth by nothing, but by prayer and fasting." This kind of miracle!

APPENDIX 2:

A LIST OF BIBLE DREAMS

Based on how the accounts of visions and dreams are worded, I see 24 distinct dreams recorded in Scripture. (I'm not including anything in this list that the Bible calls a vision.) 17 are found in the Old Testament and 7 are recorded in the New Testament.

Here is a list of dreams that are seen in Scripture.

OLD TESTAMENT DREAMS

1. Abraham falls asleep during an encounter with God. In Genesis 15, Yahweh confirms His covenant with Abram and gives him the prophecy and promise that Abram's descendants will spend 400 years in afflictions before spoiling their captors and being delivered from their bondage.

2. Abimelech is warned by God. In Genesis 20, Abimelech encounters God in a dream and is warned not to touch Sarah because she is Abraham's wife. Abimelech maintains his innocence in a conversation in the dream.

3. Jacob dreams at Bethel. In Genesis 28, Jacob dreams of a ladder that reaches up to Heaven and sees angels ascending and descending on it and Yahweh at the top. God confirms His Abrahamic covenant with Jacob.

4. Jacob dreams of being blessed with spotted livestock. In Genesis 31, Jacob receives a word of wisdom on how to deal with Laban's unfair business practices.

5. Laban is warned in a dream to leave Jacob alone. (Genesis 31:24)

6. Joseph dreams of stalks of wheat bowing down. In Genesis 37 Joseph dreams that as he and his brothers work in a field, their stalks of wheat gather around his and bow down to it.

7. Joseph dreams of the sun, moon, and stars bowing down to him. In Genesis 37, Joseph tells Jacob of this dream and Jacob is offended as he interprets it to mean that the whole family is bowing down to Joseph in his dreams.

8. Pharaoh's cupbearer shares a dream with Joseph. In Genesis 40 the imprisoned personal cupbearer of Pharaoh shares a dream he had and Joseph interprets it as a sign that he will be reinstituted to his former position within three days.

9. Pharaoh's baker shares a dream with Joseph. In Genesis 40, the imprisoned baker to Pharaoh shares a dream with Joseph, who interprets it to mean that the baker will be executed in three days.

10. Pharaoh dreams of cows. In Genesis 41, Pharaoh has two dreams. The first is that seven skinny cows appear to seven fat cows and swallow them up.

11. Pharaoh dreams of grain. The second of Pharaoh's dreams is that seven skinny ears of grain eat up seven fat ears of grain.

12. Gideon hears the Midianite dream. In Judges 7, an anxious Gideon is led of the Lord to sneak to the enemy camp where he hears two Midianites recount a dream that prophecies Gideon's victory.

13. Solomon receives an opportunity from the Lord in a dream. In 1 Kings 3, the Lord visits Solomon in a dream and offers Solomon a choice of blessings. Solomon's wise response pleases the Lord and leads to his receiving all three blessings.

14. Eliphaz receives a vision of the night. In Job 4, Job's friend recounts a revelation he received in the middle of the night.

15. Nebuchadnezzar is troubled by his dream in Daniel 2. Ultimately Daniel recounts to him his dream about a giant statue and interprets it for him as a revelation of the kingdoms of this world.

16. Nebuchadnezzar is judged in a dream In Daniel 4, Daniel interprets that Nebuchadnezzar's dream of a tree being cut down is a warning of judgment from God against the king's pride.

17. Daniel has his own dream about four beasts. In Daniel 7, the prophet dreams of four beasts that are metaphors for the empires that will rule over the Jews until the Messiah comes.

NEW TESTAMENT DREAMS

1. Joseph is comforted in a dream that Mary is carrying the Messiah. In Matthew 1:20, an encounter with an angel alleviates Joseph's agony over Mary's pregnancy.

2. The magi are warned in a dream to avoid Herod. (Matthew 2:12)

3. Joseph is instructed in a dream to move to Egypt (Matthew 2:13-15)

4. Joseph is told in a dream to return to Israel. (Matthew 2:19-21)

5. God warns Joseph in a dream to avoid Judea. (Matthew 2:22-23)

6. Paul has a vision in the night of a man of Macedonia asking him to come. (Acts 16:6-11)

7. The Lord encourages Paul in the night by a vision to continue his work in Corinth. (Acts 18:9-11)

THE REVELATION 2-3 PROPHECY MODEL

Here are 10 questions that members of The Father's House and other Spirit Forward churches regularly ask the Lord on behalf of others. They were derived from Revelation 2-3 and they help us to prophesy like Jesus. The one who desires to prophesy sits before the Lord, asks Him these questions about an individual or group, and then writes down what they think they hear the Lord saying. We have found over the years that the Lord is pleased to answer some or all of these questions for the edification, exhortation, and encouragement of His people.

1. Which aspect of God's character or name are You wanting to reveal to _____ in this particular season of life?

As the Lord Jesus addressed each of the churches in Asia, He began with a carefully chosen aspect of His own character or name that He wanted each church to focus on. In like manner, we have found that in every season of life, God is revealing an aspect(s) of His character or name to individuals, churches, nations, and generations. It may be a characteristic like compassion, power, love, holiness, etc. Or it may be one of His many titles or names like Healer, Shepherd, Warrior, Prince of Peace, or Abba.

2. What good works, qualities, or behaviors do You want to affirm?

Jesus loves to affirm His people through the gift of prophecy. We all want to know that our good works, qualities, or behaviors are seen and appreciated by the Lord. Functionally, these words of knowledge give the recipient a reason to believe a prophetic word about the future that otherwise would not be immediately verifiable.

3. What lies, strongholds, or sinful behaviors are You wanting to expose and help them overcome?

While having our sins exposed can be unsettling, it's actually very encouraging to know that Jesus is not leaving us to suffer in our sin. When the Spirit exposes something in our life that is destructive, it's because He is prepared to bless us with the grace and power necessary to overcome.

4. What trials or challenges might this person be facing?

The gift of prophecy can be used to prepare God's people for storms and trials on the horizon. We see this in Revelation 2-3. Jesus gave some of the churches in Asia an indication as to what trial(s) they would face in their next season of life. Why would He do this? He did it to take the sting of surprise out of the trial. So often that is what shakes us and causes many to despair and give up.

5. What blessings are coming for them to experience?

Seeing what blessings are coming will produce hope in the heart of a believer. Much of the Christian life is coming into the inheritance that Jesus died to give us. The Spirit uses the gift of prophecy to forecast specific blessings and to get believers into a position to receive those blessings. It may be a financial blessing, a healing, a restored relationship, an increase in spiritual gifting, a long awaited breakthrough, or any other form of favor with God and man.

6. What promise(s) do you want this person to hold onto right now?

The Lord has deliberately committed Himself to hundreds and hundreds of promises in the Scriptures. Why did He do this? To reveal His trustworthy character to us. He makes promises so that His people will stand on them, act on them, see them come to pass, catch a fresh revelation of His faithfulness, and then tell others of His goodness. Identifying which promise to stand on in this season is a wonderful function of prophecy.

7. What verse(s) of Scripture are you revealing for encouragement, obedience, or instruction?

There are more than 31,000 verses in the average English translation of the Bible, and the Spirit loves to use the gift of prophecy to highlight and empower a particular verse. The written Word of God is incredibly powerful, but it has zero effect unless it is understood and used. The soul-converting, eye-enlightening, sin-cleansing, way-warning, heart-purifying, soul-rejoicing power of the Bible belongs to those who know it and use it!

8. What Biblical account or character does this person need to hear about or remember right now?

Jesus used several biblical examples when addressing the churches in Asia, including Jezebel, Balaam, Balak, David, and Satan. Sometimes a biblical character or story can help to frame a prophetic word, reveal a strategy of the enemy, or be instructive in a variety of other ways.

9. Jesus, what do you want to show me?

Prophetic words come to those who take the time to listen with their spiritual ears and visions come to those who take the time to look with their spiritual eyes. Practically this would look like closing your eyes and waiting to see if Jesus shows you a picture or scene inside your imagination. This is how most of the prophets in the Old Testament received information from the Lord, and it is a way that He is still pleased to communicate today.

10. Father, what do you want me to say?

This question takes into consideration the fact that the Lord may want to say something to the person that doesn't fall under the category of the previous nine questions. Asking this question is like handing the Spirit a blank sheet of paper and saying, "Is there anything I've missed?" We have some amazing testimonies of things the Lord has said in response to this particular question. Sometimes He saves the best for last!

(Thank you to Jerod Long for writing this and allowing me to use it in this book.)

SUGGESTIONS FOR FURTHER READING:

CHAPTER 1

Holy Fire by R.T. Kendall

Unspeakable Joy by Martyn Lloyd-Jones

There is More by Randy Clark

Understanding Spiritual Gifts by Sam Storms

The God I Never Knew by Robert Morris

Deeper Experiences of Famous Christians by J. Gilchrist Lawson

CHAPTER 2

They Speak With Other Tongues by John and Elizabeth Sherrill.

The Beauty of Spiritual Language by Jack Hayford.

The Beginner's Guide to Spiritual Gifts by Sam Storms.

Chasing the Dragon by Jackie Pullinger.

The Language of Heaven by Sam Storms.

CHAPTER 3

The Case for Miracles by Lee Strobel

Christ the Healer by FF Bosworth

The Essential Guide to Healing: Equipping All Christians to Pray for the Sick by Bill Johnson and Randy Clark

CHAPTER 4

Systematic Theology by Wayne Grudem

Understanding Four Views on the Lord's Supper by Moore, Hesselink, Scaer, and Baima

The Power of Communion by Beni Johnson

Understanding the Lord's Supper by Bobby Jamieson and Jonathan Leeman

CHAPTER 5

The Biblical Guidebook to Deliverance by Dr. Randy Clark.

Understanding Spiritual Warfare by Dr. Sam Storms.

Defeating Dark Angels by Dr. Charles Kraft.

The Handbook for Spiritual Warfare by Dr. Ed Murphy.

Spiritual Warfare by Dr. Karl Payne.

CHAPTER 6

Fathered by God by John Eldredge

Experiencing Father's Embrace by Jack Frost

The Father Heart of God by Floyd McClung Jr.

CHAPTER 7

Two Hours to Freedom by Dr. Charles Kraft.

Transforming the Inner Man by John Loren & Paula Sandford

A Guide for Listening and Inner-Healing Prayer by Rusty Rustenbauch

CHAPTER 8

Total Forgiveness by R.T. Kendall

Forgive by Timothy Keller

Forgiving Forward by Bruce and Toni Hebel

CHAPTER 9

How to Hear God, by Pete Grieg

Designed to Dream Journal, available at www.fathershouse.tv/store

Hearing God through Your Dreams: Understanding the Language God Speaks at Night by Charity Virkler

Dreams and Visions by Tom Doyle

CHAPTER 10

Seeing is Believing by Gregory Boyd

The Veil by Blake Healy

CHAPTER 11

Prophetic Integrity by R.T. Kendall

Surprised by the Voice of God by Jack Deere

ACKNOWLEDGMENTS

To my Spirit Forward Ministry supporters,

Thank you for believing in these stories and joining me in being hungry for more. God is doing big things through each of you.

To every pastor who calls me a friend,

May God bless your families and ministries with wave after wave of continual love, favor, and power as you advance the Kingdom. Thank you for enduring and persevering.

To the members of The Father's House of West Chester,

Being your pastor for nearly a decade has been one of the great privileges of my life. Seeing God transform you and your families into Spirit-filled, passionate Jesus-followers has just made me hungrier for the Lord. Your stories deserve their own book. Maybe one day, a few of us will sit down and write it. Until then, your lives serve as visible epistles, letters to those around you that the God of Elijah is still answering prayer and baptizing living sacrifices with holy fire. Thank you for loving me and my family and following us as we followed Jesus. You have endured a season of pruning. I can't wait to see the harvest that is to come for you!

Jerod and Candice Long,

You are Jesus-loving disciples, prophetic voices, and dear friends to Candace and me. Thank you for walking so much of this journey with us. You've been strong for us in seasons of weakness and allowed us to do the same for you. May God grant you every desire of your heart as you endeavor to build His Kingdom.

Dad,

As a child, I saw you love your family, serve the poor, be a committed friend, and follow Jesus. As a man, I'm trying to do the same.

Thank you for all that you've taught me. I love you.

Mom,

Every morning, I read the Word and talk to the Lord. This is a testament to the consistent, passionate, lifelong walk you've had with Jesus. You've modeled consistent pursuit and humble dependence through the ups and downs of life. It has made it easy for me to try and do the same. You're not just a committed Christian but also a committed, loving mother. Thank you for your love and support. I love you.

Kenny, Chloe, Clarke, and Claire,

There was a time in my life when I would have seen the stories I've told in this book as being impossible. As my faith has increased, my eyes have been opened more and more to the goodness of God. I pray that you will live lives full of "impossible" stories of God's love and power and will walk in great intimacy with the Father of Lights, the Glorious Son, and the Comforting Spirit. I love each of you. Your simple faith continually reminds me of the joy that Father God finds in His children. Being your Dad is indescribably awesome. I'm so proud of each of you.

Candace,

The greatest love stories are the ones about two people whom God has joined together who walk narrow paths, endure bitter storms, and traverse vast wildernesses —always together. I always want to be with you, and you've made it clear that you always want to be with me. It doesn't get any better than that.

Loving you has taught me more about my capacity to love God than any other person or book ever could.

I love you…more.

ABOUT THE AUTHOR

Ken Schaap is a church planter, teacher, and third-generation pastor. He served as the Academic Vice President at a Bible College before planting and leading The Father's House in West Chester for ten years. During that time, Ken also founded Spirit Forward Ministries, a ministry that helps believers walk in relationship and power with the Spirit of Jesus through conferences, podcasts, and team-led prayer rooms. He and his wife Candace have four children and are currently preparing to plant a new church in Northwest Indiana.